The Art of Being Cool:

The Pursuit of Black Masculinity

Dr. Theodore S. Ransaw

Front cover illustration by Damon Stanford

First Edition, First Printing

Printed in the United States of America

ISBN #: 1-934155-76-4

ISBN #: 978-1-934155-84-4

Dedication

This book is dedicated to the ancestors that have come

before me. It is also dedicated to my grandfathers,

my grandfather's brother, my father,

my uncles, my pastor, my sensei

and all of my coaches.

Contents

Foreword

Robert L. Green, PhD

Dr. Theodore Ransaw's book identifies the major cultural and educational obstacles that limit the life opportunities of young African American males and offers solutions that are based on curricula reform and the dissemination of a more positive interpretation of popular Black male culture. In essence, he is urging us to include and affirm representations of Black achievement in schools and to harness the more progressive hip-hop messaging with mentorship to inform young Blacks that it is "cool" to be "smart."

Dr. Ransaw posits that school systems have been punishing Black youth for society's failure to engage and educate. He notes the combination of a decrease in school spending in poor neighborhoods and policy-related increases in school suspensions, expulsions and placement in behavioral schools, has paved the way for the school-to-prison pipeline. He argues that the poor academic performance of African-American boys and young men stems partly from alienation from curricula that has not represented historic realities in America and the world—from indentured white servitude in the American colonies to Black achievement in ancient African civilizations. This, Dr. Ransaw shows, is compounded by one version of hip-hop culture that discourages intellectual achievement and encourages Black males to be over-sexed and engage in illegal activities.

However, the book notes there is another strain of hip-hop culture that motivates achievement. If that aspect of popular culture is promoted with the help Black male mentors—fathers, grandfathers and uncles—in tandem with curricula reforms, dramatic change is possible. One of Ransaw's messages sums up how short-term Black macho thinking can be transformed into a longer term achievement ethos—masculinity is a pursuit, not a destination.

This is a book that educators, sociologists, psychologists and law enforcement personnel should read to understand the potential impact of curricula, mentorship and achievement values on the culture of Black male youth.

Dr. Robert L. Green is Dean and Professor Emeritus of Urban Affairs Programs at Michigan State University, former President of the University of the District of Columbia in Washington, and former Dean of the College of Urban Development at Michigan State University. Dr. Green worked for Dr. Martin Luther King, Jr., 1965-1967, as Education Director of the Southern Christian Leadership Conference.

Acknowledgments

I am grateful to Dr. Robert L. Green, Dean and Professor Emeritus, of the Urban Affairs Programs at Michigan State University, for his inspiration. I am also indebted to Dr. Porter L. Troutman, professor of education at University of Nevada-Las Vegas (UNLV) and Director of UNLV's Center for Multicultural Education, who gave me examples to follow of what good mentorship can do for willing mentees. I would also like to thank Dr. Rainier Spencer, Director of Afro-American Studies at UNLV who helped me create the masculinity class in the first place.

Most importantly, I would like to thank the men and women of my Afro-American Masculinity class who gave their instructor the opportunity to learn from them. Much of the information contained in this book came from their inspiration.

Introduction: Better, Faster, Harder—Stronger

Masculinity is not a destination but a pursuit.

If I read one more blog, tweet, journal post or book about masculinity and the need for men to show more emotion I'm going to cry. I mean, come on, the solution to men and masculinity is just to show more emotion? That's the answer? It seems to me most of the writing out there is by emotionally tortured men or women who have been mistreated by men. There is more to masculinity than the need for men to be emotional. It's not that men don't show emotion. (Have you ever seen men watching a football game or losing money on the stock exchange?) Men do show emotion every time their son does something just like them or when their daughters wear their first prom dress—or go to the prom with the wrong type of boy. Men do indeed show emotion; we just do it our own way. Also, those who seem to show a lot of emotion is not an admission that a man is gay.

While there is nothing wrong with being gay, and there have certainly been more than a few men who have not done what they should have been doing in regards to treating women with respect, I think it's time for people to hear from someone with a different perspective of masculinity.

I'm all for men becoming more aware and responsive to others but to be honest, those who need emotional and physical support come to men for strength as well as sensitivity. Privately demonstrating that you know how to cry is not going to get you ahead in the boardroom. To be clear, showing emotion, especially in front of other men, is not the key to masculinity. We do need information to help men (including gay males) understand how to work, function and live among men. I include gays for two reasons: gay men need to know about the rules and constraints of masculinity just as much as straight men. Also, what people consider effeminate behavior is not an indicator of being gay any more than acting what people consider to be overly masculine an indicator of being gay.

Manhood to me is about the choices you make on your own. Masculinity is largely about choices that others have made for you and how you embrace them. Manhood is based on efficacy; masculinity is socially constructed. While manhood and masculinity are related, this book is about masculinity. Black masculinity, which has a unique way of affecting Black manhood,

The Art of Being Cool

has its own set of social perceptions and attitude. Masculinity is about being better, faster, harder—stronger. It is an inner circle of competition and support, rivalry and brotherhood, a sense of power and a source of self-restraint. Never fully achieved, masculinity is an art form and a pursuit, not a destination. Black masculinity is a journey of self-discovery toward being a man.

In this book, I will focus mainly on the educational aspects of Black males and two underlying results: why the art of being cool is important to us, and how the art of cool is developed. Some would call it the psychology or philosophy of being cool. However, there are some physical aspects to the art of cool as well.

For example, I remember a conversation we had in class in grad school. The professor asked who played high school football. I raised my hand and enthusiastically told my jersey number when asked. The professor was making a point about how much high school sports plays a role in identity formation. While one female student mentioned that high school sports were not a big deal at her high school, another said that high school football was the entire way of life at her high school. An openly gay male spoke about how hard he and others had worked in high school to make sure posters to support the football team were made and hung up before every game. He mentioned that high school football was important at his high school but he wasn't affected one way or the other; he went to all the games just for fun. "We were busy working to make sure the school looked nice and the team was well represented. The football players walked around like they were better than us."

I was surprised and hurt. While we went to different high schools in different states, I hadn't even considered that a group of students made signs before every game in an organized fashion. I was unaware of how much hard work others had put in. I told him, "We didn't think we were better than you, we didn't know that you existed."

If you didn't play sports, or didn't try out for the team, if you were a male we didn't even see you. Not because of our elitism, it's just that sports was our world. And let me tell you, playing on a sports team does not make your life easier. It's not like someone waves a magic wand, you make the sports team and then your life is a piece of cake. You have to really work hard to make the team—any team. Once you make the team, then you have to work hard to be a starting player. Most players work hard to play both offense and defense. Then you have to work hard to be the team captain. Then you have to work hard to be all-city, then all-state, then given status on a national list of excellent athletes.

Introduction: *Better, Faster, Harder—Stronger*

The truth is the inner circle of masculinity is continuously competitive. I cannot speak for other schools, but at my high school if we bullied anyone, we had to run laps with truck tires around our heads. Not car tires, the big truck tires. (By the way, one lap constituted running up and down the stairs of the bleachers.) But that was back in my day. Today, high school coaches are not allowed to make players run laps for punishment. Students also aren't allowed to stand up for themselves in school anymore when being bullied—another aspect of proving one's masculinity from my past. I remember a student who took something from me and I confronted the student directly to give it back or else. I was suspended for three days because the vice principal said that any player in or out of a uniform can't even appear to do anything inappropriate. These modern day changes in behavior may be part of the symptoms surrounding the emerging awareness and increased incidents of bullying in America. But I digress. We were too busy competing, against each other for a spot on the team and competing against the other teams to think we were better than anyone else, let alone bullying anyone.

We did think we were better than other teams. So did most everyone else at our school. It was part of the campus culture. We played pranks against other schools, and they played pranks on us, but nothing like the type of bullying we see today. We represented the whole school and on some occasions we represented the entire city, and if we were lucky we represented the entire state. We felt like winners and people liked that about us, that their favorite teams whom they have rooted for all season were winners. Being winners makes everybody feel good about themselves and the choices they make in life. People really want to see children they know win in sports competitions. It makes them feel good about themselves and their communities. People do not like it when their high school sports teams lose, especially the big games. A dropped ball, a missed score or even a minor mistake often makes you the target of ridicule by the entire school or at least is seems that way. This two-sided coin of competing hard to be a winner at sports and avoiding what feels like awful ridicule if the opposite happens and defeat is the outcome is a large part of developing masculinity among quite a few adolescent males. For many American males, not just African Americans, playing sports is the last opportunity for someone other than a family member to guide you through personal and physical development.

Mentorship

Once I entered graduate school I was fortunate to have a Black male faculty adviser, Dr. Porter Troutman. He guided me through my PhD program and offered tips and advice about securing a job after I graduated. Dr. Troutman also extended opportunities for professional development, including workshops and conference presentations. Also, I have had priests and pastors look after me as an altar boy and as an acolyte, and I've been mentored informally by Boy Scout leaders, coaches, and even a sensei. However, I realize that I may have benefitted from opportunities that others may not have experienced. Therefore, it is incumbent on me to share what little I can. Someone did this for me and it changed my life.

This element in the development of African American masculinity emerged in my presence in 2007, during the first-ever Afro-American masculinity class offered by the Afro-American Studies Program in the Interdisciplinary Studies Department at University of Nevada-Las Vegas (UNLV). Dr. Robert Green, who served as the head of Dr. King's education task force at Southern Christian Leadership Conference agreed to be our guest speaker. He was so inspirational that the majority of my students volunteered to attend a weekly meeting with at-risk Black boys at an urban school in the area.

At first glance, the project seemed like a great idea and was met with enthusiasm by all who were involved and interested. However, I realized that just showing up at a public school to talk to at-risk students was insufficient; we needed some type of structure. What were my university student mentors going to do when they got there? How were we going to assess improvement, how were we going to hold both my students and the mentees accountable? What were the legal ramifications of a university/ school district partnership? This book discusses many of the issues and theories that went into the process of discovering what it's like to implement a meaningful African-centered mentorship that focuses on African American masculinity.

Overview

The Art of Being Cool contains nine chapters. Each chapter addresses a facet of African American masculinity. For example, "Chapter I: Race, Fear, and Economics" extends a classroom discussion my students and I undertook surrounding Black masculinity and the election of the first African American U.S. president. Typically I begin my lectures with a nonracial, economic perspective of slavery and gradually move toward how slavery reinforced racism. For me, the 2012 presidential election has exposed an often overlooked aspect of racism, economic oppression. Using terror management theory (TMT), this chapter looks at how fear and the term "Black" has been used to overshadow the fact that many European immigrants were not better off than most slaves in the formative stages of America and have remained, in many ways, as economically vulnerable to systemic oppression as they did more than 200 years ago. I assert that racism toward Blacks is often a reflection of Whites' fear of economic loss of unearned privileges.

"Chapter II: Black Males and Literacy" focuses largely on the literature review used to create the curriculum in the aforementioned mentorship program among my students at UNLV. In general, schools are failing Black boys. Boys are being placed on suspension and expelled more than girls and are more likely to have lower reading scores. However, *suspension rates are even higher while reading scores are even lower for Black boys.* Parents, teachers, and educators have been struggling for decades to find solutions to these problems. Many studies have advocated for gender relevant literature for boys to increase interest in reading. Many more studies have advocated the need for culturally competent content in literacy curriculum to reach African American students. However, research has not bridged the gap in exploring the benefits of combining gender relevant and culturally competent curricula. Using Connell's (1987) concept of hegemonic masculinity, I argue for a gender relevant and a culturally competent literacy reform that affirms Black boys' gender *and* culture.

"Chapter III: The Art of Being Cool" stems from a discussion during a conference session on preliminary research about mentorship. Here I explore the main thesis of the book, the art of being cool—the attempt to balance academic capital and social capital. Educators, employers, and volunteer organizations have struggled for years to find the best approaches to foster positive mentor/mentee relationships. Part of that discussion has centered on effective pair bonding and affinity building during mentorship. However, I suggest there are other measures for positive mentor/mentee interactions that have yet to be explored. The purpose of the mentorship program was to increase literacy and math competence while decreasing behavioral problems using the *cool factor,* embodied by a relatable and approachable mentor who helps mentees to balance their academic capital and social capital. In essence, success in school both socially and academically for all boys is the art of being cool.

"Chapter IV: Black Males and the School-to-Prison Pipeline" features startling research that leverages this argument: The link to incarceration stems from prenatal care all the way to underemployment and unemployment, during and after prison. Modern society has been struggling with social, civil, and moral issues pertaining to finding the most effective way to teach and guide children to discover a better future.

Those issues include finding the best way to educate our youth to help advance society and administering the best way to discipline students who disrupt society. Public education and the juvenile justice system are the two most popular methods in the United States. The result of primarily using these two methods has been a decrease in school spending, and an increase of school suspensions that typically leads to Black males' incarceration both as juveniles and as adults. Third- to sixth-grade reading levels and state corrections' budget cuts in education for juvenile and adult inmates—which would reduce recidivism and improve opportunities upon release—are among the challenges facing Black males in prison and juvenile corrections facilities.[1] Once adults are incarcerated, they potentially wind up providing free labor for the public sector agencies that had originally failed to provide them an education to become productive citizens in the first place. Unfortunately, these appalling trends have affected families with low social economic status and minoritized students. Chapter IV provides a snapshot of the literature that combines to assert there is a school-to-prison-to-incarceration-to-enslavement-to-forced labor pipeline fully functioning in the U.S., and offers possible cost-effective solutions to dismantle it.

"Chapter V: Black Males, Media, and Myths" centers on the hours of research I conducted creating the African American Masculinity class. This chapter utilizes a blended theoretical approach of critical race theory, in which the focus is on historical influences of myths and legends in forming male identity and uses postcolonial theory to examine current ideas that are influenced by both unconscious and conscious residual memories. Chapter V also focuses on an emerging approach called prolepsis where the future is dealt with as if it were occurring today.[2]

"Chapter VI: Hip-Hop and Masculinity" focuses on research for the other Afro-American Studies class at UNLV I taught, on Afro-American music and culture. Hip-hop has become a powerful force voicing the pain, struggles, disappointments and triumphs of masculinity, not just in America but around the world. I argue that hip-hop is a global, modern rite of passage, providing adolescents space in which to create, experiment and perform ideas of identity that preserve cultural identity. As the world has become increasingly Westernized, formal manhood rituals have become abandoned, leaving those caught between the transition from youth and adulthood looking for a voice. Using the theoretical lens of rites of passage, separation, *marge* (also known as *limen* or threshold), and aggregation,[3] research suggests that adolescents from the Americas, Germany, parts of Asia, Australia and Africa have created their own ways of defining manhood through the vocal transmission of hip-hop.

"Chapter VII: Hip-Hop Pedagogy" grew from two academic gatherings. The first was my presentation at the 2009 National Educating Black Boys Conference in Las Vegas, Nevada with my faculty mentor Dr. Porter Troutman. At the end of the 20-minute presentation of a paper I co-wrote with Dr. Troutman, the audience was so interested in the topic of hip-hop's functionality as an education tool that we fielded questions for 45 minutes! The second intellectual gathering was at a Literacy Research Association (LRA) Conference where I co-presented with my dissertation chair, Dr. Thomas Bean. After Dr. Bean and I presented a co-authored book chapter about gender and partial reconstructions of African American boys in literature,[5] someone asked about correlations to hip-hop and literacy. Hip-hop has been blamed for everything from school behavioral problems to low academic outcomes. Critics assert that youth who listen to hip-hop suffer from increased sexual activity, drug and alcohol abuse, and increased arrests. I argue that hip-hop is a cultural phenomenon that can be used positively and effectively to communicate educational instruction for multiple learners. By using the language, personal experiences, and cues from the urban environment, hip-hop can help students become self-motivated and construct knowledge on their own terms. This constructivist approach applies to today's generation in particular and Black males specifically.

"Chapter VIII: Black Male Privilege" is my humble attempt to advance theories started by African American theorists Jewel Woods and L'Heureux Lewis.[4] Black male privilege (BMP), a phenomenon where Black men center all engage in discourse on oppression directly around their own concerns, has been discussed in terms of outcomes but not the systematic religious influences that created them. In Chapter VIII, I use postcolonialism and critical race theory to examine the origins of BMP by exploring four religious narratives: the creation story, the expulsion from the paradisiacal Garden of Eden, the curse of Ham, and the biblical commandment not to lie with a man as you do a woman. Since religion is typically more influential for African American social identity than for other ethnic groups, grounding conversations of Black masculinity around tangible frameworks that illuminate how religion has influenced patriarchy in general and BMP in particular fills previous gaps in discussions of Black masculinity.

The Art of Being Cool

"Chapter IX: Black Grandfathers, Fathers, and Faith" is a summary of the insights I gleaned from interviews I conducted for my dissertation. Using interviews of three African American grandfathers and eight African American fathers, I explore the way fatherhood and spirituality intersect, make relationships meaningful, and provide grounding among African American grandfathers and fathers.

Special Features

The Appendix is one of the book's two special features. There, I examine some gender- and culturally-specific elements of style, fatherhood, and education. In an informal survey, I discovered that roughly half of my male Black students did not have anyone to teach them how to shave, and hardly any knew how to tie a necktie. This section offers a few tips on selecting a suit, dining out, and maintaining an adult's fully functioning lifestyle; gives advice on things freshmen in college should know during what is likely their first time away from home, and provides a few other practical tidbits. Another special feature of the book is the inclusion of reference lists at the end of every chapter, which reinforce much of the research and related literature that became foundational to my exploration of African American male sexuality.

Personal Bias

As I write this, I recognize that I sit in a privileged and uncommon chair as an African American male who has always had an involved father, who is close to two uncles, and who has vivid memories of both grandfathers and even fond memories of my grandfather's brother—many of whom you will see photographs of in this book. I fully realize that my experiences may not only be uncommon for my ethnicity but for most American men as well. I was born in a predominately African American, middle-class neighborhood on the South Side of Chicago. Shortly afterward my family moved from a predominately African American neighborhood to the mostly White country of England. This transition from a Black neighborhood to a White culture and country enabled me to experience being the "other" for the first time.

As a result, I have always sat as an outsider looking in, both as an African American who has had strong fathering influences throughout his life, and as an American who has lived and attended school in another country and culture. This has given me a hyper-awareness of being a Black male. Other than when I was very young, most of my experience has been as the only person of my culture and gender in class, both as a student and later as a professor. I, like many other Black males have had to pursue the never ending goal of continuously attempting to balance one's social capital with one's academic capital. That is essentially the art of being cool.

Chapter I: Race, Fear, and Economics

On top of a hill called "Class"
Looking at another hill called "Race"
Or the other way around.
It is hard to tell which hill is higher.
Henry Louis Gates,
Thirteen Ways of Looking at a Black Man, 1998

One hundred years later, the Negro lives on
a lonely island of poverty in the midst of a vast ocean
of material prosperity. It is obvious today that
America has defaulted on this promissory note
insofar as her citizens of color are concerned.
Instead of honoring this sacred obligation,
America has given the Negro people
a bad check, a check which has come back
marked insufficient funds.
Dr. Martin Luther King, Jr.
"I Have a Dream," Washington, DC, August 28, 1963

The Art of Being Cool

Introduction

There is something different about seeing President Barack Obama step off Air Force One in his custom-tailored designer suit. President Obama is cool. Whether in a meeting at the White House or just hanging out with his wife and kids, President Obama has a distinctive mannerism that some would call "swag." That is what they are calling cool nowadays, swag. President Obama's cool swag is not that surprising. When he ran for his first term in office, his campaign theme was change. Both literally and rhetorically, President Obama represents change. Not only does he look different from presidents before him, he acts differently than most other previous U.S. presidents. However, change is not something that everyone can accept. While proponents have hailed Obama's first successful presidential election as historic (Klein, 2008), opponents felt the election signaled a downfall for American society: "When the masses look at the paper and truly realize they have lost their own country" (Potok, in Clarence Page, 2008). Just a few weeks after his second successful run for president, residents in more than 29 states filed petitions to secede from the United States (Huffington Post, 2012). All of this happened before President Obama could give his second term inaugural address. While some states like Texas are known for trying to secede since the Union's inception, it is easy to conclude that many of the other states' representatives that filed petitions oppose President Obama for something more than his politics, such as race. In my opinion, President Obama represents more than just the first African American U.S. president. He depicts both an unrepresented race as well as an often unrepresented class.

Please do not get me wrong; there are many who are not happy with President Obama's White House politics, Blacks included. Examples of the latter include television and radio host Tavis Smiley, Professor Cornel West and Professor Michael Eric Dyson. However, much of the opposition toward President Obama is based on issues pertaining to the overwhelming influence of the ruling class. Take for instance the televised presidential debate in 2012 between Barack Obama and Mitt Romney. During and after the debate, Romney associated himself with the powerful elite and bourgeois ruling class of America. At the time of the debate he was estimated to be worth more than two billion dollars (Harris, 2007). On the other hand, Obama made clear from his descriptions of his upbringing—the son of a single mother, raised in modest circumstances, already detailed in his books such as *Dreams from My Father[1]*—that he was associated with everything that presidential hopeful Romney was not: someone who represents the common people as well as the poor. Obama was deemed so likable by the common people that during a debate in South Carolina in 2012, Gingrich called him "the food stamp president" (Adair & Holan, 2012).

Chapter 1: Race, Fear, and Economics

Class and Economics

Although he was once a state legislator and U.S. senator, President Obama's generational family earning and income were not the same as other senators or members of the U.S. House of Representatives. Sixty percent of the U.S. Senate and more than one out of three House members are millionaires (Sklar, 2010). The amount of wealth of the ruling class such as senators and congressmen is a significant factor in American politics, since after adjusting for inflation, workers earn less today overall than they did in 1956 (Sklar). This means the definition of poor in America also includes the working class. For Blacks in America wealth per capita is three-fifths that of Whites (Sklar)—interesting since before the Civil War Blacks were once considered worth three-fifths that of Whites.

Class and Education

The wealthy live in better homes and better neighborhoods and consequently, due to higher property taxes, have more money to spend for better quality schools, and can and do pay higher salaries for teachers and principals. The per pupil spending disparity between affluent public schools and poor public schools makes it easier to import Asians or even Africans to America than it is to send a Black kid from Compton to graduate school (PBS, 2012). However, the gap between standardized test scores of affluent and low-income students is double the testing gap between Blacks and Whites (Tavernis, 2012). In America, the number one indicator of success in school is family income and parents' education level (Zorn, et al., 2004). Not only do wealthy parents have more money to spend on books, tutors, and SAT/ACT test preparation, they also most likely have a higher education level from which to draw when they help their children with their homework. In other words, class is just as much a criterion for behavior as is thinking.

Meredith Phillips, an associate professor of public policy and sociology at the University of California, Los Angeles, used survey data to show that affluent children spend 1,300 more hours than low-income children before age 6 in places other than their homes, their day care centers, or schools (anywhere from museums to shopping malls). She found by the time high-income children start school they have spent about 400 hours more than poor children in literacy–related activities (Tavernis, 2012). Clearly, poverty and the gap between the wealthy and ruling class is not just about race. However, for many in the United States, it is easy to associate people of color with poverty, especially African Americans.

Poverty in America is associated with people of color because people of color are viewed as lazy and dependant on the government. Romney has said, "When I'm president I plan to work closely with the black community to bring a sense of pride and work ethic back into view for them" (Romney in Wood, 2012). Romney has also suggested, "Forty-seven percent of Americans

The Art of Being Cool

are dependent on the government and believe that they are entitled to health care, food and housing" (Romney in Wood). Romney's comment was so unpopular that many felt that he was out of touch with most Americans. In fact, Romney was not out of touch with the wealthy in America, especially the American White wealthy. The gap between wealthy Whites and people of color in America grew more than 20% since 2012 (Sklar, 2012). Many of those Whites became wealthy during the slave era. This intimate familiarity with those who were enslaved in America has left a lingering impression with those who were members of the ruling class of the time. Many wealthy Whites like Romney feel they can relate to African Americans in today's society because their families probably once owned slaves.

> However, just because they were freed over a century ago doesn't mean they can now be freeloaders. They need to be told to work hard, and the incentives just aren't there for them anymore. (Romney in Wood, 2012)

Perspectives similar to Romney's are symptomatic of many Americans. Our defining marker of race, class and poverty in America is slavery. If you are White in America and associate yourself with wealth, and you associate people of color in America with poverty, listlessness and slavery, then a Black president represents what is wrong with America—change in the wrong direction.

As the PBS documentary *Race 2012* asserts, America is becoming more non-White than ever before (PBS, 2012). This browning of America is underscored with the second term election of a Black president. American social roles based on race which used to represent class are starting to change in ways that are related to far more than just racism. For many, new technologies, new markets, new economies, in short, differences in American worldviews on almost every scale means a change of previous American norms. This change has caused some to be fearful of what represented the American way of life. The changing relationships to race, poverty, and class—which give clues to social status—have been causing a panic in America.

Theoretical Framework

Using TMT, terror management theory (Solomon, Greenberg, & Pyszczynski, 1991), I will explore how terror is related to class and the association of class to race in America. This perspective is especially important to the self-development, perspective, and perceptions of Black males in America. Since social roles are culturally biased and heavily influenced by self-esteem, TMT posits that when people are reminded of extreme change, such as the change of social roles or even death they turn to extremes to protect themselves (Pyszczynski, Greenberg, & Solomon, 2003).

4

Chapter I: Race, Fear, and Economics

Since social roles like class are determined by one's culture, terror about losing social status affects both Blacks and Whites.

Privilege, by its very nature when confronted with the existence of another culture, causes fear. This occurs not just because of its differences, but because the confrontation can represent a clash between different worldviews and perceptions that forces a re-examination of self. Since all cultures are socially constructed, a new or different culture represents a possible new standard of behavior, a threat, or death of self-esteem. Cultural change represents a form of cognitive dissonance or cognitive dissemblance (Piaget, et al., 1995) that has the potential to change social roles. Everything from a personal worldview to one's self-esteem is affirmed, created, and destroyed by cultural constructs. A different form of behavior or an acknowledgment that another culture exists can represent death. A culture constructs symbols and themes that represent its members' worldview, and in essence these constructs bolster the individuals' esteem within that society. Therefore, to protect society, a threatening culture requires new rules and regulations to protect the self-esteem of the original culture.

Breen (2012) assures us that was not always the case. In the early part of Virginian history, poor Whites and poor Blacks banded together to overthrow their oppressors. Founded in 1607, Jamestown, Virginia was a company before it became the center of a colony. The first English-speaking Blacks in that part of the country were indentured servants in 1619, along with many Whites. Slavery as we know it was not established in Virginia until 1640. Prior to that date, poor Whites in Virginia were not better off than most Blacks. There is even evidence that Whites and Blacks slept together, ran away together, and protested against their overseers' maltreatment together (Breen). In fact, under the leadership of Nathaniel Bacon poor Whites and Blacks expressed their anger about unfair labor treatment and government control when they set Jamestown on fire in 1676. The rebellion was quashed by British troops.

This event suggests that slavery was just as much about separating poor Whites and Blacks under the guise of race as it was about class. In other words, indentured White servants were persuaded to believe, "You may be poor, but you're not a ni-**" as an expression goes which has held currency for many generations since the 1600s. In fact, even before the precolonial era rich Whites enslaved Native Americans and purchased White slaves (Cavanaugh, 2012). Around the same time that Virginia was starting to recognize slavery, 550,000 Irish were killed and 300,000 of them were sold into slavery to the English during the Cromwell Reign of Terror during the 1650s. In fact, more Irish were sold as slaves to the American colonies and plantations from 1651 to 1660 than the total existing "free" population of the Americas! (Cavanaugh)

What I am suggesting is that slavery was initially based more on class than it was about race. For example, Wall Street was an area for slave auctions before it became associated with the New York Stock Exchange and the global stock market. Before Lehman Brothers Investments was founded in New York, the Lehman family made their money as cotton brokers in Alabama. The Morgan Family of JP Morgan Chase, Wachovia Bank of North Carolina, and Aetna Insurance all made their fortunes from selling insurance to slave owners. Race was used as a device to shroud the minds of White Americans into thinking that class was insignificant compared to race. But that has not been the case. For Whites in America, at every turn including American language, purchasing fashion, shopping at convenience stores, even the presidency has become more colorized than ever before. And if some of the changes are bad, such as the economy and politics, and those changes are represented by people of color, then race has a terrorizing influence. For many, the fear of losing America is based on the fear of others—those who are not Whites—despite the fact that America has always been an interracial place.

Lynchings

For Blacks who were enslaved in America, TMT was used in a different way. I can think of no other method of terrorizing Americans that's more effective than lynching. Lynching is the second level and perspective of TMT. Whereas fear of death by the loss of culture was used for non-wealthy Whites in America, lynching was used to cause the fear of physical death among Blacks.

It should be kept in mind that lynching was typically a Southern American Christian practice; before 1930, most of those lynched in the United States were European Americans. In 1891, 11 Italians were lynched in New Orleans. Italians were also hung in Louisiana, Mississippi, Florida, Colorado, Kentucky, Illinois, Washington, and New York between the years of 1885 and 1915, some 50 killings in all (Pacchioli, 2004). At the time, European Americans of White Anglo-Saxon Protestant descent believed they were not only superior to Blacks but also most other Whites. America was the last country in the Western world that practiced lynching (Patterson, 1998). Used as a form of terrorism toward African Americans, lynching was often followed by burning the body.

The practice of lynching was organized and planned weeks in advance, sometimes even before a victim was chosen (Patterson). Displaying a highly ritualized choreography (Brundage, 1993, p. 36), lynching was often done on trees found on church property. It was not uncommon to burn African American churches before and after lynchings. "Trees are powerful symbolic objects, universally associated with both sacred and profane myths and rituals" (Patterson, 1998, p. 205). Trees in Christianity are symbols of the cross on which Christ—the second Adam—sacrificed his

Chapter I: Race, Fear, and Economics

body. This Christian myth stems from a legend recounting that Adam's son placed a seed in his throat when he died—hence the phrase, Adam's apple. The seed grew into a tree whose branches were used for everything from the staff of Moses, to the wood used in one of King Solomon's temples. The wood from the tree was also used to crucify Christ and placed on Mount Golgotha, the same spot where Adam was buried (Every, 1970). Participants in a lynching were sacrificing their most prized property, a Black man, in a ritual to honor God and in turn, gain God's blessing. To them lynching was a gift exchange that brought magical transference of inalienability, common in cultures that value property and ownership of animals. The stock in this case was the Black man, later sacrificed after death by burning his body (Patterson, 1998). In many ways lynching represents sacrificial purification of the lynchers who have no choice but to offer the victim's body as payment to preserve their way of life.

Similar to the burned offering on altars, sacrifice and smell were important to God, who seemed to be aware of scent. All offerings of sacrifice were to be placed on an alter and burned, with the blood sprinkled against the altar. Moses instructed his followers to make a "burnt offering, a food offering, an aroma pleasing to the Lord" (Leviticus 1:3, NIV). If you were White, the odor and sweat of the Black man's skin were the only way of distinguishing and defining one's sense of self-worth versus that of the Negro (Patterson, 1998). White Southerners' fear of losing jobs to slave labor and immigrants was the beginning of latter-day reactions to affirmative action (Katznelson, 2005; Marshall, 1967).

Immediately after the Civil War, a free slave was feared and thought of as a domestic enemy, especially in the South. Wood (1968) adds evidence to this in a reprinting of the new first commandment for anti-abolitionists: "Thou shalt hate the Nigger with all thy heart, and with all thy soul, and with all thy mind and with all thy strength" (p. 36). He further offers an antebellum view of African Americans as rescued and lifted from the wilderness and savagery through slavery, leading to the idea that Afro-Americans were unredeemable, unchangeable savages who were a threat to civilized southern life (Wood). The surefire way to cleanse the southerner and to protect the southern way of life was a sacrifice and offering to the Lord in the form of a lynching. These lynchings and later the cross burnings after the end of slavery, were often presided over by White clergymen. Fundamentalist preachers and Klokards (national lecturers hired by the Klan, most of them ministers) were involved in the conspiracy of lynching invoking the Bible to justify Black subordination. These preachers not only tolerated the sacrifices of lynching but actively incited many of them (Patterson, 1998). This gave legitimacy to the claim that the ritualistic sacrifice of lynching was done in the name of God.

The Art of Being Cool

With no refuge from religion or society, African American men historically have worn stoic unemotional masks of seeming invulnerability to hide the stark realities of their past. If you are an American of African heritage, you know that someone in your past most likely was enslaved and was either victim of or saw firsthand the lynching of your people. These are the racial memories of your past (Jackson & Richardson, 2003). Although all African Americans can suffer from the veil of historical depression (Brown, 2000), because of both European and African Americans' views of Black masculinity, boys are more likely than girls to be discouraged from seeking any help, and are often punished for doing so (Stafford, Freeman, & Vianden, 2010). It is no wonder that African American men suffer from chronic depression. Also, Black men live nearly seven years less than other racial groups and experience higher mortality rates in every leading cause of death (Arias & Smith, 2003). Many of these causes of death can be linked directly to Black male depression.

This section has explored the relationship between slavery, lynching, and residual depression. Before the Civil War, antebellum lynching was used to deter slaves from escape. After the Civil War, lynching was used to prevent Black men from miscegenation with White women. Terrorism directed toward Americans of African descent is one of the reasons for Black depression. This depression is reflected in the declining mental health, decreasing physical well-being, and interrelationship problems of Black men in America.

In sum, TMT has affected Blacks by manipulating their fear of death in a way that influences their self-esteem. Without the ability to earn the income to buy property on a widespread basis or merely purchase one's own home, it's hard to build wealth. And it is impossible to vote to change these things if you are not recognized as a citizen because of voting restrictions—some of which remain influential because they're connected to incarceration. However, survivors do learn composure, self-control, and resolve.

Cool

After the experience of slavery, Blacks have remained endowed with self-resolve and resistance. This combination of attributes that Blacks have shown in their personal and collective existence—what we can call "coolness"—stems from a powerful influence known as *ashe* (De La Cancela, 1994; Bascom, 1969). *Ashe* (pronounced ash-heh) is a Yoruba term from West Africa that is related to character. Someone who has *ashe* has the power to make things happen despite the odds. In other words, *ashe* can be a source of inner strength; a nonviolent, confident, cool form of resistance against oppression (De La Cancela; Bascom). Despite the fact that

Chapter I: Race, Fear, and Economics

a person of African heritage often represents race as well as class, rejecting your heritage means believing that you are restricted to a sub-social class. Giving up your Blackness means that you give up what helped us to survive—an inconceivable response in the eyes of many Blacks. The mask-like response to oppression is fabricated to defend against total disintegration and loss of individual and communal self (De La Cancela, 1994).

A number of authors, including Majors and Billson (1992) have explored the "cool pose" or persona of being cool that is so often exemplary of Black males. Where I step away from that conversation centers on a focus of cool as a form of social capital rather than solely cultural. I assert that being cool is an art form that serves as a bridge between social classes more so than an aesthetic of resistance. The art of being cool requires balancing one's social capital with one's academic capital.

References

Adair, B., & Holan, A. D. (January 17, 2012). Is Obama really the "food stamp president"? Fact-checking the S.C. debate. *It's all politics*. NPR. http://www.npr.org/blogs/itsallpolitics/2012/01/17/145332032/

Arias, E., & Smith, B. (2003). Deaths: Preliminary data for 2001. Hyattsville, MD: *National Center for Health Statistics*.

Bascom, W. R. (1969). *The Yoruba of southwestern Nigeria*. New York: Holt, Rinehart and Winston.

Breen, T. (2012). Timothy Breen on the relationship between black slaves and white indentured

servants. *Africans in America*. PBS. Retrieved November 16, 2012 from http://www.pbs.org/wgbh/

Brown, D. F. (2003). Urban teachers' use of culturally responsive management strategies. *Theory into Practice, 42*(4), 277-282.

Brown, T. N., et al. (2000). "Being Black and feeling blue": The mental health consequences of racial discrimination. *Race & Society, 2*(2), 117-131.

Brundage, W. F. (1993). *Lynching in the new South: Georgia and Virginia 1880-1930*. Urbana: University of Illinois Press.

Cavanaugh, J. (2012). Irish slavery. *Race and History News and Views*. Retrieved December 26, 2012 from http://www.raceandhistory.com/cgibin/forum/webbbs_config.pl/noframes/read/1638

De La Cancela, V. (1994). "Coolin": The psychosocial communication of African and Latino men. In D. J. Jones (Ed.), *African American males: A critical link in the African American family* (pp. 33-45). New Brunswick: Transaction Publishers.

Douglass, F. (1845, 1982). *Narrative of the life of Frederick Douglass*. New York: Penguin Books.

Eagly, A. H., Wood, W., & Diekman, A. B. (2000). Social role theory of sex differences and similarities: A current appraisal. In T. Eckes & H. M. Trautner (Eds.), *The developmental social psychology of gender* (pp. 123-174). Mahwah, NJ: Erlbaum.

Every, G. (1970). *Christian mythology*. London: The Hamlyn Publishing Group Limited.

References

Gates, H. L. (1998). *Thirteen ways of looking at a Black man.* New York: Vintage Books.

Harris, M. (2007). Millionaires-in-chief. CNN Money. Retrieved December 26, 2012 from http://money.cnn.com/galleries/2007/moneymag/0712/gallery.candidates.moneymag/6.html

Heilman, M. E., Wallen, A. S., Fuchs, D., & Tamkins, M. M. (June, 2004). Penalties for success: Reactions to women who succeed at male gender-typed tasks. *Journal of Applied Psychology, 89*(3), 416-427.

Jackson, R., & Richardson, E. (2003). *Understanding African American rhetoric: Classical origins to contemporary innovations.* New York: Routledge.

Katznelson, I. (2005). *When affirmative action was white: An untold history of racial inequality in twentieth-century America.* New York: W. W. Norton.

King, M. L. (August 28, 1963). I have a dream. Washington, DC.

King, M. L. (2005). I have a dream [DVD video]. Oak Forest, IL: MPI Home Video.

Klein, J. (2008). Obama's historic victory. *Time.* Retrieved December 27, 2012 from http://www.time.com/time/politics/article/0,8599,1700132,00.html

Ladson-Billings, G. (1994). *The dreamkeepers: Successful teachers of African American children.* San Francisco: Jossey-Bass.

Majors, R., & Billson, J. (1992). *Cool pose: The dilemmas of Black manhood in America.* New York: Lexington Books.

Marshall, F. R. (1967). *Labor in the South.* Cambridge, MA: Harvard University Press.

Pacchioli, D. (May 1, 2004). *Dark Legacy.* University Park, PA: Penn State University. Retrieved December 26, 2012 from http://www.news.psu.edu/140775/2004/05/01/research/dark-legacy/

Page, C. (August 17, 2008). Obama vs. bigots and "swift books" [electronic version]. *Real Clear Politics.* Retrieved December 17, 2008 from http://www.realclearpolitics.com/articles/2008/08/obama_vs_bigots_and_swift_book.html

Patterson, O. (1998). *Rituals of blood: Consequences of slavery in two American centuries.* New York: Civitas Books.

PBS. (2012). *Race 2012: A conversation about race and politics in America.* Retrieved December 27, 2012 from http://race2012pbs.org/

Piaget, J., Gruber, H., & Voneche, J. J. (Eds.). (1995). *The essential Piaget* (100th anniversary ed.). New York: Jason Aronson.

Pyszczynski, T., Greenberg, J., & Solomon, S. (2003). *In the wake of September 11: The psychology of terror.* Washington, DC: American Psychological Association.

Residents in more than 30 states file secession petitions. *Huffington Post.* http://www.huffingtonpost.com/2012/11/13/petition-to-secede-states_n_2120410.html

Sklar, H. (2010). Imagine a country. In Paula Rothenberg (Ed.), *Race, class and gender in the United States* (pp. 307-316). New York: Worth Publishers.

Solomon, S., Greenberg, J., & Pyszczynski, T. (1991). A terror management theory of social behavior: The psychological functions of self-esteem and cultural worldviews. *Advances in Experimental Social Psychology, 24,* 93–159.

Stafford, A., Freeman, J. P., & Vianden, J. (May, 2010). Helping college men transcend the "boy problem:" A call to union and activities professionals. *The Bulletin, 79*(3). Retrieved December 27, 2012 from http://www.acui.org/ publications/ bulletin/article.aspx?issue=22642&id=12587

Stark, R. (2007). *Sociology* (10th ed.). Belmont, CA: Thomson Wadsworth.

Tavernis, S. (2012). Education gap grows between rich and poor, studies say. *The New York Times.* Retrieved December 27, 2012 from http://www.nytimes.com/2012/02/10/education /education-gap-grows-between-rich-and-poor-studies-show.html PBS. (1985, 2003). A class divided. *Frontline.* Retrieved November 16, 2012 from http://www.pbs.org/ wgbh/Wood, F. G. (1968). *Black scare: The racist response to emancipation and reconstruction.* Berkeley: University of California Press.

Wood, P. (2012). Peter Wood on the shift from indentured servitude to lifelong slavery. *Africans in America.* PBS. Retrieved November 16, 2012 from http://www.pbs.org/wgbh/

Wood, S. (March 13, 2012). Mitt Romney: I can relate to Black people because my ancestors once owned slaves. *Freewood Post.* Retrieved December 27, 2012 from http:// www.freewoodpost.com/2012/03/13/

Zorn, D., et al. (March, 2004). *Family Poverty and Its Implications for School Success: Issues Facing Cincinnati's Families* (Executive summary). Cincinnati: University of Cincinnati Evaluation Services Center.

Chapter II: Black Males and Literacy

I had to realize when I was very young that

I was none of those things that I was told I was....

I had been invented by white people.

James Baldwin, "A Talk to Teachers,"

Saturday Review, December 21, 1963, p. 44

"If you teach that n*** how to read, there would be no

keeping him. . . . He would at once become

unmanageable, and of no value to his master."

Frederick Douglass, *Narrative of the Life of*

Frederick Douglass, 1845, p. 78

The minute they see me, fear me,

I'm the epitome—public enemy.

Public Enemy, "Don't Believe the Hype,"

It Takes a Nation of Millions to Hold Us Back, 1988

The Art of Being Cool

Introduction

Being cool often entails social capital for Black boys, but this hardly ever translates into academic capital. That may be one of the reasons why Black boys and boys in general drop out of school more than girls. In the United States, graduation rates from public high schools are low for males, 65% (Greene & Winters, 2009). In fact, girls outperform boys in almost every related category of reading (Organization of Economic Cooperation and Development, 2006), a contributing factor for the low percentage of male graduation. Graduation rates for minoritized males are even lower, 55% for African Americans and 53% for Hispanics (Greene & Winters, 2009). In 2003, 2005, 2007, and 2009, Black boys scored the lowest in reading proficiency in fourth grade, and in 2009 Black males scored 42% lower than White males at meeting college reading level benchmarks (Lewis, Simon, Uzzell, Horwitz & Casserly, 2010). Nationally, 84% of Black boys who cannot read at grade level have dropped out by 12th grade (Children's Defense Fund, 2007). In Las Vegas, less than a third of Black boys graduate from high school on schedule (Jackson & Holzman, 2010).

Low graduation rates for Black boys are reflective of at least two national trends, Black boys placed on suspension and Black boys placed in special education. Although Black students made up only 17% of the overall population in 2000, they accounted for 34% of all suspensions (U.S. Department of Education, 2001). The majority of those suspensions were Black boys. African Americans make up 41% of the students in special education programs, and 80% of Black special education students are male (Kunjufu, 2010). One might argue that Black males are just not interested in reading, as well as more likely to be disruptive in school and possibly developmentally delayed, because Black boys go to the same schools as Black girls and both groups have majority White female teachers (Kunjufu, 2010). It is more likely, however, that Black boys are at risk because of culturally and socially constructed factors such as race and gender. Shirley Heath (1983) asserts that different communities read texts in complex but different ways, which supports this reasoning.

Anti-Masculine Pedagogy

While the low reading levels for Black boys and the trend of Black boys being placed on suspension and in special education may not be based on conscious racism, it is clear, Brown and Davis (2000) assert, that schools are not meeting the social and developmental needs of African American males. White, middle-class female teachers are simply not ready to deal with the social, cultural, and gender issues of, as Collier put it, other people's children (2007). It is typical for a White female teacher to hear a Black boy say, while crossing his arms and with a scowl on his face, *"No white*

Chapter II: Black Males and Literacy

woman can teach a young Black man, so you might as well forget trying" (Sleeter, 2010, p. 2).

Not just in the above example but in general, education is not a warm and inviting place for cultural interaction between Black boys, White teachers, and society, and often serves as a forum to disrupt cultural synchronization (Irvine, 1990). The communication styles of African Americans are seen as high-keyed, animated, and confrontational by White norms (Kochman, 1981). Bowles and Gintis (1976) assert that schools have a hidden curriculum of promoting White middle-class culture as superior and normal. What *is* normal behavior? Normal behavior is based on what is considered proper (Glasser, 1984) and more often than not, normal behavior is White behavior.

What is the solution? Hilliard (1995) suggests that the experience of Black boys needs to be understood within the relational context of their experience in America. I assert that Black boys are both Black and male; therefore, their problems in literacy development are not based solely on culture and gender constraints, but the fluid and interconnected boundary between the two. In other words, Black boys suffer from both gendered and cultural nihilism in school. To elucidate this gendered and cultural exclusion, this chapter will draw from hegemonic masculinity as conceived by R. W. Connell (1995; 1996; 2002).

Definition of Literacy

While there are many definitions of literacy, for the purpose of this chapter, literacy will be defined as the ability to read and write with understanding a simple statement related to one's daily life. It involves a continuum of reading and writing skills, and often includes basic arithmetic skills (UNESCO, 2000).

Theoretical Framework

Connell developed her theory on hegemonic masculinity while researching class structure and education inequities, two issues specifically pertinent to masculinity and Black boys. Connell's main perspective is that current social and power conditions are based on patriarchal norms that represent the desired ideals of a small and select group of men (Connell, 1995; 2002). Connell's theory of masculinity is sometimes referred to as hegemonic masculinity, as her ideas are concerned with both hegemonic and non-hegemonic masculinity. This is similar to Bourdieu's (1986) ideal of cultural hegemony. The three-volume *Prison Notebooks* by Antonio Gramsci (1891-1937) informed Connell's view of hegemonic masculinity as two-way and simultaneous, a practice that forms and is formed by structures that are appropriated and defined (Connell, 1995).

Put in another way, hegemonic masculinity is a practice that is being recreated under constantly changing conditions, including resistance by subordinate groups (Wedgwood, 2009), and is not a fixed biological behavior (Bean & Harper, 2007). I take that as evidence that Connell's hegemonic masculinity is suitable as a frame to study the interrelated issues of Black boys, literacy, and culture.

Need for Masculine Literacy Practices

Hegemonic masculinity is central to many of the struggles boys face in literacy (Martino & Kehler, 2007). In fact, there has been concern about the feminine and frilly content of elementary education since the late 1960s (Connell, 1996). Boys are at a disadvantage with feminized forms of teaching more likely to reward quiet sitting and noncompetitive behavior (Martino, 2007). From as early as 1966, research has suggested that males work better in competitive environments and girls prefer cooperative environments (Connell, 1996). Males tend to extract, seeing things in components and isolation, and girls tend to embed, looking at things holistically. Boys are more impulsive and girls are more reflective (Head, 1996). As a result, boys often reject reading, considering it for *nerds* and *uncool* (Brozo, 2005), and outside the construction of masculinity (Archer & Yamashita, 2003). For Black boys in particular, reading a book is considered acting White (Buck, 2010). Any action that is not considered appropriate based on White norms of hegemonic masculinity is viewed as social misbehavior.

Interrelated Nature of Culture, Literacy, and Discipline

This does not mean that Black boys cannot behave, but that the interpretations of what is appropriate behavior are based on relational issues or context (Sheets & Gay, 1996) that are not in line with Black masculine identity (Noguera, 2003). Black children, especially Black male children, are used to being active, audience participatory, and exuberant, characteristics that are outside the norm for proper "White" behavior (Collier, 2007). In fact, Ferguson (2000) suggests that negative beliefs about African American men, in this case boys, are so ingrained that their childlike behavior is painted as sinister.

Even the walk or stroll—the tendency of African American males to swagger—has forced teachers to consider Black boys more likely to attain lower academic achievement, to be in need of special education services and to act aggressively (Neal, 2003). It may be that the proclivity to place Black boys on suspension and in special education programs is an attempt to deculturize them to behave in White hegemonic- framed norms (Spring, 2001). Corrective behavioral problems based on White cultural norms are a form of both cultural genocide (Hilliard, 1976) and cultural imperialism (Lynn, 2002). These cultural deficits are reinforced in the lack of culturally inclusive reading curriculum and in the use of culture to discipline unwanted behavior.

Chapter II: Black Males and Literacy

Behavior expectations are so rigid and racially-driven that Black boys are often called out in class as examples of inappropriate behavior for White students (Collier, 2007). It is not farfetched to wonder if the perceived discipline problems of Black boys by White teachers is based on Black boys' fear of being called out and used as an example when they are not proficient readers. Additionally, many Black boys feel that their teachers expect them to fail (Tatum, 2008). Indeed, some teachers feel that Black boys are so far beyond help that they are beyond love (Duncan, 2002). A child without love learns to fend on its own.

Black boys construct their own definition of Black masculinity based on what they expect from themselves to survive (hooks, 2004; Franklin, 1985). This definition of Black masculinity is often conceptualized as a *cool pose* (Majors & Billson, 1992), or a withdrawal from study and immersion in sports. Cool pose is the appearance of being resilient, relaxed, confident, and emotionally detached (Hecht, Jackson, & Ribeau, 2003) for psychological, emotional, and physical survival. Conforming to non-masculine activities like studying and paying attention in school just is not cool. The school is not the only institution involved in the construction of masculinity. The media also have a role (Connell, 1996).

Influences of Alternate Texts

Rap music reflects a rebellion against the attempt to control Black masculinity in the home and on the street (Blair, 2004). The hyper-visibility of minoritized ethnic young men as objects of concern is contrasted with their invisibility in academic literature (Alexander, 2003). This often leaves them little choice but to search for masculinity in other forms of literacy such as hip-hop.

One conundrum in contemporary hegemonic masculinity is the fact that some young white men are emulating "hard" Black masculinity for its association with sexual prowess (Back, 1996). In Connell's words regarding peer culture, "[B]lack masculinity that is familiar in white racism—and has now been seen by young black men (for instance in rap music) is a source of power" (1996, p. 219). Interest in rap music is also an indicator of being placed in special education programs (Jackson, 1999). I assume that interest in European classical music is not an indicator of placement in special education programs. However, these hegemonic masculinities are still associated with educational failure despite their emotional and social appeal (Archer & Yamashita, 2003). This means that the appeal of rap music may be based on its ability to be a powerful alternative text of performance masculinity in a way that is gender affirming. In addition to rap and hip-hop, the performance of masculinity is often displayed in the socially and masculine affirming role of playing sports.

17

The Art of Being Cool

Influence of Sports

Not just a phenomenon related to Black boys, American sports reinforce aggressive behavior and dominating performances of masculinity (Connell, 1996). However, for Black boys, socially constricting frames of Black masculinity are so narrow that many are left with the choice of being popular or smart, since appearing smart or speaking correctly is deemed as derogatory (Kunjufu, 1988). It is much more culturally accepted for both White and Black girls to be interested in an athlete than a nerd. For Black boys in school, there are two forms of masculinity: the smart boys or academic achievers, and the cool boys, commonly known as the athletes (Connell, 1996). This fact enhances gender issues for Black boys when the idea that resistance to education is a rite of passage in the act of being considered cool. Put simply, it is more both socially and culturally accepted for Black boys to embrace masculine and socially affirming actions of rebounding off backboards than answering socially emasculating questions on the chalkboard. "Literacy education has to have a strong gravitational pull for African American male adolescents [that speaks] in their present-day contexts" (Tatum, 2008, p. 163) in order to effectively break these gendered and cultural norms.

Alternative Frameworks That Affirm Identity

There are numerous academic publications (Kochman, 1981; Duncan, 2002; Fordham, 1986; Jones & Bush, 2004; King, 2008; Murrell, 2002; Tatum, 2008) and books (Kunjufu, 1988; Ogbu, 2004) detailing the need for culturally competent content in education. There are also many books that assert the influence of gender in literacy development and literacy interest (Connell, 1996; Brozo, 2005, 2010; Greene & Winters, 2009; Head, 1996; Roderick, 2003; Smith & Wilhelm, 2002). There is even more research on the important role that both race and gender play in education (Ferguson, 2000; Archer & Yamashita, 2003; Chavous, Rivas-Drake, Smalls, Griffin & Cogburn, 2008; Collier, 2007; Green, Carl, Green, & Mount, 2010; Lewis, Simon, Uzzell, Horwitz, & Casserly, 2010; Sleeter, 2010; Tatum, 2005). However, there is hardly any research expressing the need for cultural, ethnically *and* gender competent content in literacy as a method to increase interest in reading for African American boys. In other words, previous studies have ignored racialized and gendered identities and have instead focused on comparing their academic outcomes to those of other students (Davis, 2001; Dill & Zambrana, 2009; Gilbert & Gilbert, 1998).

By their very lenses, these studies have overlooked the role culture and identity play in literacy interest. There is a need to include the voices of African American adolescent males in literacy research (Tatum, 2008). I suggest that if educators want to increase literacy in Black boys, they need to provide them with enabling texts that relate specifically to them.

Chapter II: Black Males and Literacy

Discussion

Tatum (2008) defines an *enabling text* as "one that moves beyond a solely cognitive focus—such as skill and strategy development—to include a social, cultural, political, spiritual, or economic focus" (p. 164). This perspective requires a new way of looking at literacy in a way that forces teachers regardless of race to affirm the gender and masculine identities of their Black male students. There is absolutely no research that says that only Black teachers can teach Black students to read (Tatum, 2005). This idea is supported by research that insists culturally responsive management practices can work with White teachers and African American students (Brown, 2003) and reduce problems associated with discipline. All teachers can get Black boys to respond if they incorporate culturally competent practices such as using music [hip-hop], introducing hobbies [sports], artifacts and implementing relevant storytelling teaching strategies (Shade, Kelly, & Oberg, 2004). What is needed in culturally responsive teaching is understanding the needs and experiences of students' cultural knowledge, acknowledging their prior experiences, accepting their frames of reference, and affirming their cultural learning styles to make learning relevant and effective (Gay, 2000). This can be best accomplished with literacy reform that relates to Black boys in ways that affirm both their racial and their gendered identities. In other words, books specifically targeted to Black boys can indeed get them to read, simply because the books are cool.

Cool, gender and literacy. There are at least two perspectives regarding gender and literacy. One perspective is that schooling is patriarchal, restrictive, and limiting to women. Weaver-Hightower (2003) suggest that masculinity is a defining element in education and that male dominant gender and gender roles are tied to the smooth functioning of society and consequently influence schooling. Curriculum textbooks especially depict women as limited while men are shown as leaders (Weaver-Hightower, 2009). The other perspective regarding gender and literacy is that an overwhelming number of White middle-class female teachers in American schools have feminized education for boys.

Many teenage boys are turned off to reading because it's considered "nerdy" and uncool (Brozo, 2005), and outside the construction of masculinity (Archer & Yamashita, 2003). In fact, there has been concern about the feminine and frilly content of elementary education since the late 1960s (Connell, 1996). Boys are at a disadvantage due to feminized forms of teaching that are more likely to reward quiet sitting and non-competitive behavior (Martino & Kehler, 2007). Studies show that girls outperform boys in almost every related category of reading (Organization of Economic Cooperation and Development, 2006), a contributing factor for the low percentage of male graduation. Scholars have argued both sides, some claiming that curriculum materials are weighted toward masculinity (Kuzmic, 2000). Others assert that academic materials favor girls and their interests, especially regarding literacy (Brozo, 2002; Evans & Davies, 2000; Millard, 1997).

While these two perspectives seem disparate, they share a common vantage point of hegemonic masculinity. In other words, hegemonic masculinity is central to many of the struggles boys face in literacy (Martino & Kehler, 2007), regardless of perspective. In 2003, 2005, 2007, and 2009, Black boys scored the lowest in reading proficiency in fourth grade, and in 2009 Black males scored 42% lower than White males at meeting college reading level benchmarks (Lewis, et al., 2010). This means minoritized boys are a subordinated group in regards to reading and schooling. However, there are solutions.

Cool Pedagogy

As Tatum (2008) has observed, when literacy education gives African American male adolescents content that features avenues to their context—especially in the present day—there will a strong payoff of interest. For example, it *is* possible to engage Black boys in reading by utilizing multifaceted texts such as Sharon Flakes' (2010) *You Don't Know Me* which explore complex identities of Black male masculinity. Flake allows the reader to explore multiple points of view by incorporating short stories and poems that engage different narratives. This method of combined genres highlights the "power and privilege within masculinities and recognize[s] that masculinities are complicated and multifaceted and may even be contradictory" (Wedgwood, 2009, p. 336). Put in another way, hegemonic masculinity is a practice that is constantly being recreated under changing conditions, including resistance by subordinate groups (Wedgwood), and is not a fixed biological behavior (Bean & Harper, 2007).

I advocate for more culturally and gender enabling texts such as *Monster* (Myers, 2001) and *You Don't Know Me* that move beyond "unrealistic evaluations of deficiency towards any other group that is not White or middle class based on White males as the control group" (Padilla in Banks, 2004, p. 129). Even White males who are not middle class often have trouble identifying with White males who are (Roediger, 2005).

Tatum (2008) defines an *"enabling text* as . . . one that moves beyond a solely cognitive focus—such as skill and strategy development—to include a social, cultural, political, spiritual, or economic focus" (p. 164). This idea is supported by research on culturally responsive management practices by White teachers of African American students (Brown, 2003) that can reduce problems associated with discipline. These practices include the use of hip-hop music, encouragement for participation in sports and other

Chapter II: Black Males and Literacy

hobbies, the presence of culturally competent and uplifting artifacts, and relevant storytelling strategies as part of teaching (Shade, Kelly, & Oberg, 2004). What is needed in culturally responsive teaching is understanding the needs and experiences of students' cultural knowledge, acknowledging their prior experiences, accepting their frames of reference, and affirming their cultural learning styles to make learning relevant and effective (Gay, 2000). For example, teachers who show appreciation of "high-and-low" languages in ways that are inclusive of varying degrees of cultural, ethnic, and social status (Saville-Troike, 1989) may find that this cultural modeling form of African Americans' socially accepted learning methods could eliminate the negative stigma of a student standing out for being smart (Lee, 2000) and reduce behavioral problems. Helping boys to utilize cultural identifiers they are familiar with in ways that affirm their identity may be a key to reducing behavioral problems.

Cool's Relationship to Discipline

With this in mind, if minoritized boys like school and like their teachers, but are still having behavioral problems in school, it may be that behavioral problems are linked to negotiating their cultural identity regarding successful life outcomes. Simpson (1996) attests that boys like reading about subjects that relate to social power and being successful.

Boys are interested in reading about subjects that are relatable to social power and becoming successful (Simpson). If texts or curriculum do not convey learning in a way that helps minoritized boys to capitalize on their individual forms of identity and social capital, then what is the motivation for them to read much less do well in school? Social capital by its very definition means the ability of actors to secure benefits by virtue of membership in social networks or other social structures (Portes, 1998). Students who attend schools that do not allow them to use the social capital they are familiar with may feel they lack purpose. Covington's (1998) self-worth theory of motivation describes the competitive nature of academics and creates an atmosphere where students are motivated to avoid failure, not to achieve success. Protecting pride and self-worth becomes the only viable solution in no-win situations (Martin, et al., 2003). However, atmospheres where schools make students feel accepted, valued, and encouraged have higher academic achievement (Faircloth & Hamm, 2005; Honora, 2003). I take this to mean the positive results from the mentorship program stem from the atmosphere the mentors created, which encouraged the mentees to find pride and self-worth in their own defined sense of academic identity.

To summarize, the previous section provided brief definitions of mentorship and being cool and how these are related to social capital, academic capital, and the praxis of cool. Also, we explored how cool affects the classroom with regard to discipline. In the next section, we'll look at using a theoretical framework to analyze the research behind the ailments that affect minoritized boys.

Fast Break to Literacy Reform

The following section is a list of recommended gendered and culturally affirming books, what I call cool books, for Black boys and Black adolescent males. These books were selected based on content of the material as well as the gender and culture of the main characters. For the most part, autobiographies and nonfiction historical pieces are not included in the list for young and adolescent Black males in favor of either mythical heroes or contemporary and relatable narrative-driven short stories. While this list is by no means exhaustive, it is my hope that it will encourage others to make and add on to lists like this to share with other educators.

Recommended reading for young African American boys (ages 6-12)

Kickoff! by Tiki Barber and Ronde Barber with Paul Mantell

Julian, Secret Agent, by Ann Cameron

I Like You But I Love Me, by Common, illustrated by Lorraine West

Michael's Golden Rules, by Deloris Jordan with Roslyn M. Jordan, illustrated by Kadir Nelson

We Are the Ship: *The Story of Negro League Baseball,* words and pictures by Kadir Nelson

Ain't Nothing But a Man: My Quest to Find the Real John Henry, by Scott Reynolds Nelson with Marc Aronson

Bottom of Form*Kevin and His Dad*, by Irene Smalls, illustrated by Michael Hays

Just the Two of Us, by Will Smith, with pictures by Kadir Nelson

No Boys Allowed! by Christine Taylor-Butler, illustrated by Mark Page

Recommended books for adolescent Black males (ages 13-17)

The Watsons Go to Birmingham 1963: With Connections, by Christopher Paul Curtis

Bang! by Sharon G. Flake

Chapter II: Black Males and Literacy

You Hear Me? Poems and Writing by Teenage Boys, edited by Betsy Franco

The First Part Last, by Angela Johnson

Bad Boy: A Memoir, by Walter Dean Myers and *Somewhere in the Darkness* by Walter Dean Myers

Hip Hop Street Curriculum: Keeping It Real. Chicago: African American Images, by Jawanza Kunjufu

Recommended books for teachers

Black Athena: The Afroasiatic Roots of Classical Civilization (The Fabrication of Ancient Greece 1785-1985, Volume 1), by Martin Bernal

Nile Valley Contributions to Civilization: Exploding the Myths, by Anthony Browder

Educating Black Males: Critical Lessons in Schooling, Community, and Power, by Ronnie Hopkins

Stolen Legacy, by George James

Changing School Culture for Black Males. Chicago: African American Images, by Jawanza Kunjufu

Understanding Black Male Learning Styles, by Jawanza Kunjufu,

Through Ebony Eyes: What Teachers Need to Know But Are Afraid to Ask About African American Students, by Gail Thompson

References

Archer, L., & Yamashita, H. (June, 2003). Theorizing inner-city masculinities: "Race," class, gender and education. *Gender & Education, 15*(2), 115-132.

Alexander, B. K. (August, 2003). Passing, cultural performance, and individual agency: Performative reflections on black masculine identity. *Cultural Studies/Critical Methodologies, 4*(3), 377-404.

Back, L. (1996). *New ethnicities and urban culture: Racisms and multiculture in young lives.* New York: St. Martin's Press.

Baldwin, J. (December 21, 1963). A talk to teachers. *The Saturday Review, 46*(51), 42-44, 60.

Bean, T. & Harper, H. (January, 2007). Reading men differently: Alternative portrayals of masculinity in contemporary young adult fiction. *Reading Psychology, 28*(1), 11-30.

Blair, E. (2004). Commercialization of the rap music youth subculture. In M. Forman & M. A. Neal (Eds.), *That's the joint! The hip-hop studies reader.* New York: Routledge.

Bourdieu, P. (1986). The forms of capital. In J. G. Richards (Ed.), *Handbook of theory and research for the sociology of education* (pp. 241-258). New York: Greenwood Press.

Bowles, S., & Gintis, H. (1976). *Schooling in capitalist America: Education reform and contradictions of economic life.* New York: Basic Books.

Brown, D. F. (2003). Urban teachers' use of culturally responsive management strategies. *Theory into Practice, 42*(4), 277-282.

Brown, M. C. & Davis, J. E. (2000). *Black sons to mothers: Compliments, critiques, and challenges for cultural workers.* New York: Peter Lang Publishers.

Brozo, W. G. (2005). Gender and reading literacy. *Reading Today, 22*(4), 18.

Brozo, W. G. (2010). *To be a boy, to be a reader: Engaging teen and preteen boys in active literacy* (2nd ed.). Newark, DE: International Reading Association.

Buck, W. (2010). *Acting white: The ironic legacy of desegregation.* New Haven, CT: Yale University Press.

Chapter II: Black Males and Literacy

Chavous, T. M., et al. (May, 2008). Gender matters, too: The influences of school racial discrimination and racial identity on academic engagement outcomes among African American adolescents. *Developmental Psychology, 44*(3), 637-654.

Collier, D. L. (2007). *Sally can jump but Jerome can't stomp: Perceptions, practice and school punishment.* (Doctoral dissertation, Long Beach and Irvine, CA: California State University/University of California-Irvine.

Connell, R. W. (1995). *Masculinities.* Cambridge: Polity Press.

Connell, R. W. (Winter, 1996). Teaching the boys: New research on masculinity, and gender strategies for schools. *Teachers College Record, 98*(2), 206-235.

Connell, R. W. (2002). *Gender.* Cambridge: Polity Press; Malden, Blackwell Publishers.

Davis, J. E. (2003). Early schooling and academic achievement of African American males. *Urban Education 38*(5), 515-537.

Douglass, F. (1845). *Narrative of the life of Frederick Douglass.* Boston: Anti-Slavery Office.

Dill, B. T., & Zambrana, R. E. (2009). *Emerging intersections: Race, class and gender in theory, policy and practice.* New Brunswick, NJ: Rutgers University Press.

Duncan, G. A. (May, 2002). Beyond love: A critical race ethnography of the schooling of adolescent black males. *Equity & Excellence in Education, 35*(2), 131-143.

Ferguson, A. A. (2000). *Bad boys: Public schools in the making of Black masculinity.* Ann Arbor: University of Michigan Press.

Franklin, C. (1985). The Black male urban barbershop as a sex-role socialization setting. *Sex Roles, 12*(9-10), 965-979.

Fordham, S. (1996). *Blacked out: Dilemmas of race, identity and success at Capital High.* Chicago: University of Chicago Press.

Gay, G. (2000). *Culturally responsive teaching: theory, research, and practice.* New York: Teachers College Press.

Gilbert, R., & Gilbert, P. (1998). *Masculinity goes to school.* New York: Routledge.

Glasser, W. (1986). *Control theory in the classroom.* New York: Perennial Library.

The Art of Being Cool

Gramsci, Antonio (2010). *Prison notebooks: Three-volume set.* New York: Columbia University Press.

Green, R. L., Carl, B. C., Green, K. K., & Mount, R. (2010). *The American dilemma and challenge: The African American male dropout rate.* Las Vegas: Clark County School District.

Greene, J. P., & Winters, M. (2009). *Leaving Boys Behind: Public High School Graduation Rates.* Education Working Paper Archive. Retrieved from http://www.uark.edu/ua/der/EWPA/Research/Accountability/1779.html

Head, J. (1996). Gender identity and cognitive style. In P. F. Murphy & C. V. Gibbs (Eds.), *Equity in the classroom: Towards effective pedagogy for girls and boys* (pp.59-70). London: Falmer Press.

Heath, S. B. (1983). *Ways with words: Language, life and the work in communities and classrooms.* Cambridge, UK: Cambridge University Press.

Hecht, M., Jackson, R., & Ribeau, S. (2003). *African American communication: Exploring identity and culture* (2nd edition). Mahwah, NJ: Lawrence Erlbaum Associates.

Hilliard, A. G. (1976). *Free your mind: Return to the source, African origins.* Atlanta: Georgia State University Press.

Hilliard, A. G. (1995). *The maroon within us: Selected essays on African American community socializations.* Baltimore, MD: Black Classic Press.

hooks, b. (2004). *We real cool: Black men and masculinity.* New York: Routledge.

Irvine, J. (1990). *Black students and school failure.* New York: Greenwood Press.

Jackson, J., & Holtzman, M. (2010). *Yes we can: The Schott 50 state report on public education and Black males 2010.* Cambridge, MA: Schott Foundation for Public Education. Available at http://www.Blackboysreport.org/

Jackson, J. F. (December, 1999). What are the real risk factors for African American children? *Phi Delta Kappan, 81*(4), 308-312.

Jones, R. S., & Bush, L. (2004). Leading schools through culturally responsive inquiry. In F. English, et al. (Eds.), *Sage handbook of educational leadership* (pp.269-296).

Kehler, M. (2008). The read and mis-read bodies of boys: Masculinities and critical social literacy practices. In R. Hammett & K. Sanford (Eds.), *Boys, girls, and the myths of literacy and learning.* Toronto, ON: Canadian Scholars Press.

Chapter II: Black Males and Literacy

King, J. E. (2008). *Black education: A transformative research and action agenda for the new century*. Mahwah, NJ: Lawrence Erlbaum Associates.

Kochman, T. (1981). *Black and white styles in conflict*. Chicago: University of Chicago Press.

Kunjufu, J. (1988). *To be popular or smart: The Black peer group*. Chicago: African American Images.

Kunjufu, J. (2010). Personal communication.

Lewis, S., et al. (2010). *A call for change: The social and educational factors contributing to the outcomes of Black males in urban schools*. Washington, DC: The Council of the Great City Schools.

Lusher, D., & Robins, G. (2009). Hegemonic and other masculinities in local social contexts. *Men & Masculinities, 11*(4), 387-423.

Lynn, M. (May, 2002). Critical race theory and the perspectives of Black men teaching in the Los Angeles public schools. *Equity & Excellence in Education, 35*(3). 119-130.

Majors, R., & Billson, J. M. (1992). *Cool pose: The dilemmas of Black manhood in America*. New York: Lexington Books.

Martino, W., & Kehler, M. D. (2007). Gender-based literacy reform: A question of challenging or recuperating gender binaries. *Canadian Journal of Education*, Special Issue: Guest Editors, M. Kehler & W. Martino. *Boys, Literacies and Schooling, 30*(2), 406-431.

Murrell, P. C. (2002). *African-centered pedagogy: Developing schools of achievement for African American children*. Albany, NY: State University of New York Press.

Neal, L., et al. (Spring, 2003). The effects of African American movement styles on teachers' perceptions and reactions. *Journal of Special Education, 37*(1), 49-57.

Noguera, P. A. (2003). Schools, prisons, and social implications of punishment: Rethinking disciplinary practices. *Theory into practice, 42*(4), 341-350.

Ogbu, J. (2008). *Minority status, oppositional culture, & schooling: Sociocultural, political, and historical studies in education*. New York: Routledge.

Organization of Economic Cooperation and Development (OECD). (2006). Education at a glance. Retrieved January 3, 2013 from http://www.oecd.org/edu/skills-beyond-school/educationataglance2006-home.htm

Public Enemy [Ridenhour, C., Shocklee, H., Rogers, N., & Drayton, W.] (1988). Don't believe the hype. *It takes a nation of millions to hold us back.* New York: Def Jam/Columbia/ CBS Records.

Roderick, M. (2003).What's happening to the boys? Early high school experiences and school outcomes among African American male adolescents in Chicago. *Urban Education, 38*(5), 538-607.

Shade, B. J., Kelly, C., & Oberg, M. (2004). *Creating culturally responsive classrooms.* Washington, DC: American Psychological Association.

Sheets, R., & Gay, G. (May, 1996). Student perceptions of disciplinary conflict in ethnically diverse classrooms. *NASSP Bulletin, 80*(580), 84-94.

Sleeter, C. (2010). "Why" paper exercise. In K. Koppelman (Ed.), *Understanding human differences: Multicultural education for a diverse America* (UNLV custom edition). Boston, MA: Pearson Allyn & Bacon.

Smith, M. S., & Wilhelm, J. D. (2002). *Reading don't fix no Chevys: Literacy in the lives of young men.* Portsmouth, NH: Heinemann.

Spring, J. (2001). *Deculturization and the struggle for equality: A brief history of education of dominated cultures in the United States.* Boston: McGraw-Hill.

Tatum, A.W. (2005). *Teaching reading to Black adolescent males: Closing the achievement gap.* Portland, ME: Stenhouse Publishers.

Tatum, A. W. (Spring, 2008). Toward a more anatomically complete model of literacy instruction: A focus on African American male adolescents and texts. *Harvard Educational Review, 78*(1), 155-180.

United Nations Educational, Scientific and Cultural Organization (UNESCO). (2000). *World Education Report: The Right to Education, Towards Education for All Through- out Life.* Paris: UNESCO.

U.S. Department of Education, National Assessment of Educational Progress. (2007). *The Nation's Report Card: 12th Grade Reading and Mathematics 2005.*

U.S. Department of Education. Office of Civil Rights. (2001). *Elementary and Secondary School Survey: National and State Projections.* Washington, DC: U.S. Government Printing Office.

Wedgwood, N. (2009). Connell's theory of masculinity—its origins and influences on the study of gender. *Journal of Gender Studies 18*(4), 329-339.

Chapter III: The Art of Being Cool

In both the logics of the subculture and of cool,
the more visibly a person rejects the standards
of the adult culture, the more status she or he has...
Amy C. Wilkins,
Wannabes, Goths, and Christians, 2008, p. 38

"Hip [from the West African Wolof word hepi/hipi]
is the dance between black and white—
or insider-outsider."
Joseph Leland,
Hip: The History, 2004, inside flap

The Art of Being Cool

Introduction

The impetus for this chapter stemmed from a discussion during a conference presentation of qualitative pre-test data at an international mentoring conference in Albuquerque, New Mexico. Data used in the presentation were collected from a pre-test survey regarding attitudes toward school pre-tests. Students in the mentorship program were all Black boys who were attending an at-risk school, in an at-risk neighborhood with all White teachers. The principal and teachers selected mentees based on low academic achievement, high incidences of behavioral problems, and the belief in the potential of each of the mentees in the program. All of the mentees self–reported that they like school, they like their teachers, and all but one said they felt their teachers cared about them.

The data contrast starkly with other reports which assert that White female teachers do not care about Black boys, and that Black boys do not care about school or their teachers. This begs the question: *If the mentees like school and like their teachers, why are they having behavioral problems?* Additionally, the data from the pre-test survey show that, at least initially, the mentorship program is effective in regard to increasing positive attitudes toward reading and math while decreasing behavioral problems. This prompted a second question: *Since the mentees already liked school and their teachers, what did the mentors do to get positive outcomes?* One conference audience member suggested the cool factor; i.e., since the mentors serving in the mentorship program were all college students, but still hip and cool, they were more approachable and more impactful than their teachers were. I assert that the mentors also helped the mentees find their own version of academic cool. This chapter is an outgrowth of exploring the benefits of the cool factor and begins with a series of definitions of key terms under discussion.

Definitions

Definition of Mentorship

Mentorship can be defined as assistance from influential or significant people to achieve life goals (Torrance, 1984), or as a person who teaches, counsels, or inspires. Treffinger (2003) conceptualizes mentorship as established from high expectations with mutual benefits to both the mentee and mentor. A good mentor has even been described as someone who "lead[s] students on a journey that forever changes the way they think and act, and consists of different diverse experiences" (Zipp & Olson, 2009, p. 9). Clark (1995) asserts that mentoring includes knowing how to negotiate bureaucracy and how to build and establish allies, and having the know-how to teach mentees how to read and transmit social cues. Good mentors not only help their mentees do well

Chapter III: The Art of Being Cool

academically, they also help their mentees to navigate socially. In addition, successful mentors help mentees create a plan of action or a future-plan. This idea is supported by research that suggests that future time perspectives such as life plans, encourage students to actively consider how present academic behaviors impact their ability to reach future goals and expectations, and should in turn motivate students to engage in behaviors that will increase the likelihood of reaching their goals (Adelabu, 2010).

Additionally, studies have found that African American students who report a greater focus on the future tend to earn higher grades (Adelabu; Cunningham, Corprew, & Becker, 2009; Honora, 2002). Life plans that focus on time perspectives that combine short- and long-term goals have been found to significantly influence motivation. I define mentorship as a relationship founded on the building blocks of measurable goals for the mentee such as life plans under the direction of a caring and relatable mentor.

Mentor relationships typically deteriorate because mentors fail to commit to the time and effort needed to make a difference (National Urban League, 1992). Most mentorship experiences fail because of a mismatch between the expertise of the mentor and the needs of the mentee, an inappropriate or insufficient structure in the relationship between the mentor and mentee regarding transmission of information, or a lack of an established, systematic, long-term method for engagement (Hiley, 2010). That means *successful mentorship* requires structure and planning, pre- and post-mentee training and support (Jekielek, Moore, & Hair, 2002), and presence and consistency (Ford, Harris, & Schuerger, 1993). I feel that sustained mentorship is the most effective way to deconstruct the hidden nuances of hegemonic masculinity that influence minoritized boys and create or withhold opportunities for them.

Definition of Cool

The concept of cool has been traced back to Africa (Janzen, 1972). In fact, the word "cool" stems from *ewuare,* a Yoruba term in West Africa that is often assigned to one who is crowned king (Majors & Billson, 1992). "Cool" in Africa is associated with numerous attributes such as patience, mental calmness, art, dance rituals, and most importantly, competitive environments such as elite, all-male warrior cults (Thompson, 1984).

From as early as 1966, research has suggested boys work better in competitive environments (Connell, 1996). Additionally, males tend to extract, seeing things in components and isolation. Reading is rarely competitive and hardly impulsive. As a result, boys often reject reading, considering it outside the construction of masculinity (Archer & Yamashita, 2003; Brozo, 2005). But what

31

The Art of Being Cool

is cool? Everyone knows what cool is *not*, but how do we define what *is* cool? Cool, put simply, intersects race, class, gender (Wilkins, 2008) and if I may add, social economic status, or SES. For instance, for Black boys reading a book has been described as acting White [read "uncool"] (Buck, 2010). However, it is not simply the act of reading that is uncool. Any action that is not appropriate based on White norms of hegemonic masculinity for the minoritized is viewed as uncool.

In fact, elite 19th century English masculinity was associated with "natural" mental superiority (Cohen, 1998). It is the social advantages of the upper-class White male which lead to the impression that success should appear effortless. After all, privileged men do not work hard. This holds true in life and as well as in the classroom. Reay (2004) asserts the "effortless generation of scholarship" is part of the idealized norm and adds: "For those who have prior advantage application becomes pedantry and a respect for hard work grinding, limited pettiness" (Bourdieu & Passeron in Reay, 2004, p. 36). This uncool to work discourse has become a norm among middle-class and working-class boys and is not restricted to race or ethnic group (Francis & Archer, 2005). In fact, this uncool to work hard in school phenomenon is the topic of several research articles (Epstein, 1998; Archer, et al., 2005; Francis, 1999; Francis, et al., 2009; Frosh, et al., 2002; Younger & Warrington, 2005). It has even been argued that to be a boy is to "succeed without trying" (Hodgetts, 2008, p. 476) and that academic hard work is often incompatible with "cool" masculinities in many schools (Epstein, 1998; Frosh, et al., 2002; Jackson, 2009; Younger & Warrington, 2005). Cleveland (2011) describes this behavior as part of the boy Code where males are not allowed to show emotion, look week, a sissy or to be a failure. Paying attention to a White female teacher read as the epitome of uncool to other boys as she is a member of both the oppressive race and inferior gender (Cleveland, 2001).

Definition of Social Capital and Academic Capital

In an effort to avoid being perceived as uncool, many boys who are successful in school sometimes try to make it look effortless (Jackson & Dempster, 2009). These academically successful boys are attempting to balance their social capital with their academic capital. Bourdieu (1986) defines social capital as networks and connections that can be transmitted to children. The concept of social capital includes ways in which social bonds of shared values such as trust add value to individuals and organizations (McGrath & Van Buskirk, 1996).

Social capital is intrinsically related to academic capital since schools are communal organizations (McGrath & Van Buskirk, 1996). Sullivan and Sheffrin (2003) describe academic capital as related to human capital potential, measured by knowledge and

Chapter III: The Art of Being Cool

skills reflected by education or as Bourdieu (1986) described it, the social transmission of schooling through family and culture. This balancing act, between being social and being a scholar, is an attempt to find a "middle way" between schoolwork and "cool work" (Frosh, et al., 2002, p. 205). The avoidance of being perceived as socially inept is more than just a form of social capital; it is also a matter of survival to not be bullied (Frosh, et al., 2002). Effort and diligence are associated with femininity, and femininity remains masculinity's subordinated other (Dweck, 2000).

So again, Weaver-Hightower (2003) reminds us that not only is cool transcended by race, ethnicity, and class, but by accepted norms of sexuality as well. Even the educational success of girls and women has not broken the stigma that working hard in school is for girls (Hodgetts, 2008). So in essence, the effortless demonstration of masculinity also known as being cool can be viewed as a cultural archetype (Jung, 1966), significantly intersecting class with race, sexuality, gender, and nationality (Connell, 2000), and related to ideology and interpersonal relationships in adolescent ethnic identity (Steinberg, 1993; McKenry, et al., 1989). Cool is more than not acting White; it is the performance of masculinity based on looking relaxed and effortless.

The Praxis of Cool

The art of effortless cool serves a two-fold purpose. Not working hard and looking cool is rewarded by others and affirms masculinity by avoiding femininity; and failing in the art of being cool can be attributed to a lack of effort, not the lack of ability, and any success can be attributed to effortless natural ability (Hodgetts, 2008; Cohen, 1998; Covington, 1998; Dweck, 2000). This stands in stark contrast to other perspectives of Black masculinity that merely focus on Black boys who are forced to choose between being popular or smart (Kunjufu, 1988), a thug or sellout (Groenke & Youngquist, 2011), or the frequently misinterpreted views of Ogbu (2004), that Black boys suffer from the oppositional culture and are afraid to act White. I say "misinterpreted" because Ogbu actually asserted that both societal and school discrimination, instrumental community factors such as perceptions of lack of jobs, *and* Black oppositional culture are three interrelated factors in which to examine Black students' low academic behavior. This is often described as the *cool pose* (Majors & Billson, 1992), or a withdrawal from study and immersion into sports. Cool pose is the masculine appearance of being resilient, relaxed, confident, and emotionally detached (Hecht, Jackson, & Ribeau, 2003).

These perspectives serve to reinforce the idea that resistance to education is a rite of passage for Black boys who are trying to enact coolness. However, I feel that lack of engagement in reading for Black boys is more nuanced than just the binary opposition of the smart boys or academic achievers, and the cool boys, commonly known as the athletes (Connell, 1996). I assert that different communities read texts in complex and different ways (Heath, 1983), and Black boys need to be understood within the relational context of their experience in America (Hilliard, 1995). For example, Latino boys mold themselves around the expectations set forth for them and can feel marginalized, disenfranchised, and shamed in American schools (Trueba, 1993; Valdes, 1996). The art of masking in Spanish, especially among young Latino males is called *la cara de palo* or "wooden mask" (De La Cancela, 1994, p. 33). Dr. Gilberto Q. Conchas, an associate professor of education at University of California-Irvine said, "If you're macho, you don't need to ask questions, you don't need to participate. You're in class, what more do people want from you?" (Newman, 2010). This is especially significant with regard to critical literacy as Stevens and Bean (2007) inform us: Whom made the message, what the message is trying to say, and for whom the message is intended are the lens that readers employ to decode text.

Theoretical Framework

This chapter will borrow concepts from R. W. Connell's hegemonic masculinity that is heavily influenced by Gramsci. For Connell, hegemonic masculinity is defined by idealized notions of the masculinity among White, heterosexual, and economically successful men (Connell, 1995), and ignores the oppression of other groups that do not fit. In the words of Paulo Freire, "The oppressed find in the oppressor their model of 'manhood'" (Freire, 2000, p. 46). According to Padilla (2001), the model of the elite White male is used to compare not only behavior but also White middle-class male measures of intelligence and educational outcomes. Restricting to both women and minorities, White expectations and norms for Black students often cause Black males to over-identify with being Black and embrace an Afrocentric identity as psychological protection against oppression. White, middle-class male overgeneralizations of the "norm" exaggerate the differences between groups and direct unrealistic evaluations of deficiency toward any other group that is not White or middle class based on White males as the control group (Padilla in Banks, 2004, p. 129). In other words, Black male identity is often created in comparison to and in opposition of White males. Even White males who are not middle class often have trouble identifying with other White males who are (Roediger, 2005). This in turn affects conceptions of masculinity and embodiment of fatherhood for any group that is the *other.*

At this point it is important to note that hegemonic masculinity intersects at least three other socially related theories. The first is Bandura's social learning theory (1977). Social learning theory asserts that learning is a social function comprised of attention, retention, reproduction, and motivation (Bandura, 1977), all key factors in effective mentoring. The second is social

Chapter III: The Art of Being Cool

cognitive theory (Miller & Dollard, 1941; Bandura, 1986), which views learning as a process acquired from observing the behavior of others. Successful cognitive learning, an integral part of social learning, occurs when there is close identification with the observed such as a relatable mentor. Finally, the third intersecting theory is social conflict theory by Karl Marx (1971). Social conflict theory contextualizes issues related to social classes such as competition over scarce resources, structural inequalities between groups, revolutions, and conflicts that result in violent behavior or even war (Marx). The overarching theme of these three theories is that hegemonic masculinity in some way or another situates itself around competition between the ruling class and subordinated groups.

Recommendations

Balancing cultural, social and academic capital seems to help minoritized children in school. *Cultural capital* includes cultural habits and dispositions inherited from family that are fundamental in school success (Bourdieu & Passeron, 1979). *Social capital* consists of networks and connections that can be transmitted to children (Bourdieu, 1986; Portes, 1998). *Academic capital* is related to human capital and is measured by professional knowledge and skills that are typically reflected in the level of education (Sullivan & Sheffrin, 2003). How can students obtain access to cultural, social, and academic capital? They can do so by participating in social networks (Ceballo, 2004) such as mentorship programs (Carbonaro, 1998) and having short- and long-term objectives. Details of three such objectives are outlined below.

Objective 1 – Increasing Literacy

The principal duty of the mentorship program was to provide academic, social and cultural capital through mentorship that produces college- and career-ready students. The first step in this mentorship model includes increasing literacy. Literacy, the ability to identify, understand, interpret, create, and communicate written and printed text is one of the most important keys to positive education outcomes. The importance of literacy to positive education and life outcomes cannot be overstated. "The link between illiteracy and incarceration rates is so strong that some states decide the number of prison cells to build based on fourth grade reading levels" (Trivani, 2009). To carry out Objective 1 in a mentorship program entails regularly scheduled meeting times where the mentor not only reads to the mentee but is also read to by the mentee to help evaluate listening skills and comprehension. The mentorship program looked at outcomes of Objective 1 - Improvement in Literacy based on a survey that focused on attitudes toward reading and teacher evaluations.

The Art of Being Cool

Objective 2 – Improving Math Competency

The mentorship program also was dedicated to improving math competency. According to research from Robert Green, et al. (2010), between 2007 and 2009 "African American male in mathematics passing rates (met proficiency) ranged from a high of 28.5% in 2008-09 to a low of 26.5% in 2007-08. These results are disturbing when compared to the passing rates of the [school] district (nearly 46%) and their Hispanic (nearly 35%) and White (nearly 64%) male counterparts" (p. 16). Objective 2 of the mentorship program includes mentor support of the mentee in regards to mathematical proficiency up to at least Algebra I. Algebra I is an indicator for college success among minoritized students (Atanda, 1999; Moses & Cobb, 2001).

Objective 3 – Decreasing Behavioral Problems

Fostering positive relationships in society requires culturally competent interaction. Cultural clashes based on ethnicity are often confounded by social class, resulting in unilateral comparisons between middle-class Whites and working-class African Americans, Hispanics, or even immigrant populations (Padilla, 2004). Measurements against middle-class Whites that intersect race, class, culture, and religion often create adversarial relationships. This results in the likelihood that minoritized and African American boys will be placed in detention or referred to special education based on cultural misunderstandings. Contrary to belief, most juvenile detentions are not due to violent offenses. Consequently, the more a student is placed on suspension or in detention the more likely it is that the student will drop out. "In CCSD [Clark County School District], suspensions are seen as a contributing factor to low achievement and high dropout rates observed with minority students" (Green, et al., 2010, p. 18).

Additionally, merely instilling a strong sense of ethnic identity alone is not the answer to positive outcomes in education. According to Ogbu (2004), a strong sense of ethnic identity can create a rejection against studious behavior that can be seen as "acting White". Consequentially, a strong sense of self-confidence is a greater indicator of positive educational outcomes than is ethnic identity alone. Positive interactions with an advisor or mentee are a strong predictor of academic support regardless of same ethnicity pairing. To that end, the mentorship program will engage in fostering positive interactions between mentors and mentees as well as other forms of positive interactions such as mentees' dealings with classmates and teachers. Positive interaction will be provided in the form of both structured and non-structured meetings, classroom visits, as well as tours of college campus, career day visits by various professionals, and cultural activities. Positive interaction was measured by teachers' evaluations of behavior.

Chapter III: The Art of Being Cool

Discussion

Overall, the research suggests that negative attitudes toward school, reading, and math *increased* in the mentees' self-reported surveys, while teachers' surveys of mentees suggests no significant change in reading, math, behavior, academic capital, or social capital. However, there were no significant changes in positive attitudes toward teachers, and all of the mentees expressed positive feelings toward their mentors, indicating they felt their mentors were cool. The data may be interpreted such that one-on-one mentorship may be more engaging and preferred over traditional classroom instruction. Additionally, the pre-test was administered at the beginning of the school year when the mentees had just met their teachers, and the post-test was administered after CRT testing. Perhaps the mentees had a novice's barometer of their grade-level work at the beginning of the mentorship and had test fatigue toward the end of the mentorship program.

With regard to the cool factor being interpreted as balancing academic and social capital, due to absences, expulsions, and transfers, only half of the data on the mentees could be correlated. The data collected from half of the mentees suggest that both academic and social factors had increased during the time of the mentorship program.

As demonstrated, scholars have been debating if the difficulties that Black boys are having in school are related to the dilemma of *being poplar or smart* or the lack of having positive role models. This trend of thought has been updated to include the phenomenon of *cool pose* or the *fear of acting White,* the misogynistic saturated medium of hip-hop, and the proliferation of White female teachers. However, the reasoning is the same: Black boys are struggling in school based on influences that stem from seeking social acceptance while maintaining their racial identities in school environ-ments that are not culturally or gender affirming.

Data collected from the attitude toward school pre-test of 12 mentees in an all-African American mentor program who attend an at-risk school in an at-risk neighborhood revealed they felt that school was important, felt their teachers felt good about them, and all but one felt good about their teachers. The survey indicates that the majority of the mentees liked their teachers and liked school, but disliked reading aloud and answering questions from the teacher about what they have read. All of the mentees in the mentorship program were selected based on low academic achievement, high incidences of behavioral problems, and the belief in their potential by the principal and their teachers. All of the teachers are White females. This data contrasts strongly with other reports which assert that White female teachers do not care about

Black boys, and that Black boys do not care about school or their teachers.

Based on observations, reactions, and feedback from the mentors in the program, I argue that Black boys are indeed seeking to be cool, but coolness on their terms is related to the appearance of looking effortless about academics. In other words, the mentorship program, with its group of cool, hip college students who served as mentors and helped academically struggling Black boys, also helped them to find ways to affirm their cultural and ethnic identities. This opinion is based on mentees' evaluations of mentors and teachers' evaluation of mentees' social and academic capital.

This section has discussed the results of mentees' self-reported surveys of attitudes toward school, reading, and math, as well as teachers' survey evaluations of mentees' reading, math, behavior, and social capital. The next section will describe some of the chapter's limitations and provide suggestions for the future.

Limitations

Limited Time of Mentors

Due to the college students' busy schedules, they had limited time available, especially during periods of mid-term and final examinations. Whenever mentors missed a session, incentives for program participation waned among mentors and mentees and behavioral problems increased among mentees. In addition, a mentee may have become jealous when his mentor was absent while other mentees got to have the benefit of their mentors' presence.

In-School Mentorship

Taking a mentee out of class had the benefit of allowing both the teacher and other classmates a brief period without potential distractions by students with known instances of doing so. However, this may have given the appearance of rewarding undesirable behavior. Additionally, students outside of the program may have gotten jealous.

Mentor Expertise

While all of the mentors completed at least 90 minutes of training, they were not teachers. Having examples of pertinent information to include during the one-on-one sessions and using activity sheets required a lot of practice. Additionally, effectively understanding a reading miscue analysis and math literacy teaching strategies could be challenging for subject matter specialists, let alone undergraduates.

Chapter III: The Art of Being Cool

Suggestions for the Future

Limited Time of Mentors

- Schedule alternative activities for mentees during unplanned mentor absences such as instructional videos and pre-planned activities.

- Provide an incentive for the mentor with above average attendance.

In-School Mentorship

- Have mentees bring any seatwork they are working on in school to the mentor session.

- Have the mentees report the activities completed during the mentor session, including any behavior strategies they are working on.

- Stress that participation in the mentorship program requires that mentees meet both GPA and behavior conditions.

- Provide more opportunities for successful mentee-peer interaction, such as guest speaker days where mentees and other students at the school are all in the same room.

Mentor Expertise

- Provide more instruction to mentors on implementing detailed recordkeeping for reading miscue analysis and having prepared, structured math drills for mentees.

- Give mentors examples of succinctly completed activity sheets.

- Demonstrate reading miscues to mentors as a group.

- Increase the level of accountability among mentors to include mentee absence reports, reasons for absences, and follow-up steps to take.

- Replicate this level of accountability as it regards mentors' absences, reasons, and follow-up steps to take.

References

Adelabu, D. H. (November 14, 2010). *Gender Differences Among the Psycho-social Constructs That Shape Academic Achievement for High Achieving African American Adolescents.* Paper presented at the 2010 Success Summit. Fort Lauderdale, FL: African American Success Foundation.

Archer, L., Halsall, A., Hollingworth, S., & Mendick, H. (2005). *Dropping Out and Drifting Away: An Investigation of Factors Affecting Inner-City Pupils' Identities, Aspirations and Post-16 Routes. Final Report to the Esmee Fairburn Foundation.* London: IPSE.

Archer, L., & Yamashita, H. (2003) "Knowing their limits?" Identities, inequalities and inner city school leavers' post-16 aspirations. *Journal of Education Policy 18*(1), 53-69.

Archer, L., & Yamashita, H. (2003). Theorizing inner-city masculinities: "Race," class, gender and education. *Gender & Education, 15*(2), 115-132.

Atanda, R. (Spring, 1999). Do gatekeeper courses expand education options? *Education Statistics Quarterly, 1*(1), 33-37.

Bandura, A. (1986). *Social foundations of thought and action: A social cognitive theory.* Englewood Cliffs, NJ: Prentice Hall.

Bandura, A. (1977). *Social learning theory.* Englewood Cliffs, NJ: Prentice Hall.

Bean, T. W., Dunkerly, J., & Harper, H. (2013). *Teaching young adult literature in new times.* Thousand Oaks, CA: Sage.

Bean, T. W., & Harper, H. (January, 2007). Reading men differently: Alternative portrayals of masculinity in contemporary young adult fiction. *Reading Psychology, 28*(1), 11-30.

Berrill, D., & Martino, W. (2003). Boys, schooling and masculinities. Abingdon: Carfax.

Bourdieu, P. (1986). The forms of capital. In J. G. Richardson (Ed.), *Handbook of theory and research for the sociology of education* (pp. 241-258). New York: Greenwood Press.

Chapter III: The Art of Being Cool

Bourdieu, P., & Passeron, J. C. (1979). *The inheritors: French students and their relations to culture*. Chicago: University of Chicago Press.

Boykin, A. W. (1983). On academic task performance and Afro-American children. In J. T. Spence (Ed.), *Achievement and achievement motives* (pp. 324-371). Boston: W. H. Freeman.

Brown, D. F. (2003). Urban teachers' use of culturally responsive management strategies. *Theory into Practice, 42*(4), 277-282.

Brozo, W. G. (2002). *To be a boy, to be a reader: Engaging teen and preteen boys in active literacy*. Newark, DE: International Reading Association.

Brozo, D. F. (2012). Outside interest and literate practices as contexts for increasing engagement and critical reading for adolescent boys. In B. Guzzetti & T. Bean (Eds.), *Adolescent literacies and the gendered self: (Re)constructing identities through multimodal literacy practices*. New York: Routledge.

Brozo, W. G. (2005). Gender and reading literacy. *Reading Today, 22*(4), 18.

Buck, W. (2010). *Acting white: The ironic legacy of desegregation*. New Haven, CT: Yale   University Press.

Carbonaro, W. J. (October, 1998). A little help from my friend's parents: Intergenerational closure and educational outcomes. *Sociology of Education, 71*(4), 295–313.

Ceballo, R. (2004). From barrios to Yale: The role of parenting strategies in Latino families. *Hispanic Journal of Behavioral Sciences, 26*(2), 171–186.

Clark, C. (September, 1995). Innovations in the mentoring process. *Equity and Excellence, 28*(2), 65-68.

Cleveland, P. C. (2011). *Teaching boys who struggle in school*. Alexandria, VA: ASCD.

Cohen, M. (1998). "A habit of healthy idleness": Boys' underachievement in historical perspective. In D. Epstein, et al. (Eds.), *Failing boys? Issues in gender and achievement*. Buckingham: Open University Press, 19–34.

Connell, R. W. (1995). *Masculinities.* Cambridge: Polity Press.

Connell, R. W. (1996). Teaching boys: New research on masculinity, and gender strategies for schools. *Teachers College Record, 98*(2), 206-235.

Connell, R. W. (2000). *The men and the boys.* St. Leonards, N.S.W.: Allen & Unwin.

Connell, R. W. (2002). *Gender.* Cambridge: Polity Press.

Connell, R. W. (2005). *Masculinities.* (2nd ed.). Cambridge: Polity Press.

Covington, M. V. (1998). *The will to learn: a guide for motivating young people.* Cambridge, UK: Cambridge University Press.

Cunningham, M., Corprew, C. S., & Becker, J. E. (2009). Associations of future expectations, negative friends, and academic achievement in high-achieving African American adolescents. *Urban Education, 44*(3), 280-296. doi: 10.1177/0042085908318715

De La Cancela, V. (1994). "Coolin": The psychological communication of African and Latino men. In D. J. Jones (Ed.), *African American males: A critical link in the African American family.* New Brunswick, NJ: Transaction Publishers.

Dweck, C. S. (2000). *Self-theories: Their role in motivation, personality and development.* Philadelphia: Psychology Press.

Epstein, D. (1998). Real boys don't work: "Underachievement", masculinity, and the harassment of "sissies". In D. Epstein, et al. (Eds.), *Failing boys? Issues in gender and achievement.* Buckingham: Open University Press, 96–108.

Evans, L., & Davies, K. (February, 2000). No sissy boys here: A content analysis of the representation of masculinity in elementary school textbooks. *Sex Roles, 42(3-4),* 255-270.

Faircloth, B., & Hamm, J. (August, 2005). Sense of belonging among high school students representing four ethnic groups. *Journal of Youth and Adolescence, 34*(4), 293-309.

Flake, S. G. (2004). *No boys allowed.* New York: Zenderkidz.

Chapter III: The Art of Being Cool

Flake, S. G. (2005). *Bang!* New York: Hyperion/Jump at the Sun.

Flake, S. G. (2010). *You don't even know me: Stories and poems about boys.* New York: Hyperion/Jump at the Sun.

Fordham, S., & Ogbu, J. (1986). Black students' school success: Coping with the "burden of 'acting White.'" *Urban Review, 18*(3), 176-206.

Ford, D. Y., Harris III, J. J., & Schuerger, J. M. (March-April, 1993). Racial identity development among gifted Black students: Counseling issues and concerns. *Journal of Counseling and Development, 71*(4), 409-417.

Francis, B. (1999). Lads, lasses and (new) labour: 14- to 16-year-old students' responses to the "laddish" behaviour of boys and boys' underachievement debate. *British Journal of Sociology of Education, 20*(3), 355–371.

Francis, B., & Archer, L. (2005). Negotiating the dichotomy of Boffin and Triad: British–Chinese pupils' constructions of "laddism". *Sociological Review, 53*(3), 495–521.

Francis, B., Skelton, C., & Read, B. (2009). The simultaneous production of educational achievement and popularity: How do some pupils accomplish it? *British Educational Research Journal, 36*(2), 317-340.

Franco, B. (Ed.). (2001). *Do you hear me? Poems and writings by teenage boys.* Cambridge, MA: Candlewick Press.

Freire, P. (2000). *Pedagogy of the oppressed.* New York: Continuum.

Frosh, S., Phoenix, A., and Pattman, R. (2002). *Young masculinities: understanding boys in contemporary society.* Basingstoke: Palgrave.

Gay, G. (2000). *Culturally responsive teaching: theory, research, and practice.* New York: Teachers College Press.

Green, R. L., Carl, B. C., Green, K. K., & Mount, R. (December, 2010). *The American dilemma and challenge: The African American male dropout rate.* Las Vegas: Clark County School District.

Groenke, S. L., & Youngquist, M. (April, 2011). Are we post-modern yet? Reading *Monster* with 21st-century ninth graders. *Journal of Adolescent & Adult Literacy, 54*(7), 505-513.

Guthrie, J. T., & McRae, A. (2011). Reading engagement among African American and European-American students. In S. J. Samuels & A. E. Farstrup (Eds.), *What research has to say about reading instruction* (pp. 115-142). (4th ed.). Newark, DE: International Reading Association.

Hall, R. E. (July-August, 2009). Cool pose, black manhood, and juvenile delinquency. *Journal of Human Behavior in the Social Environment, 19*(5), 531-539. doi:10.1080/109113 50902990502

Heath, S. B. (1983). *Ways with words: Language, life and the work in communities and classrooms.* Cambridge, MA: Cambridge University Press.

Head, J. (1996). Gender identity and cognitive style. In P. F. Murphy & C. V. Gibbs (Eds.), *Equity in the classroom: Towards effective pedagogy for girls and boys* (pp 59-70). London: Falmer Press.

Hecht, M. L., Jackson, R. L., & Ribeau, S. A. (2003). *African American communication: Exploring identity and culture* (2nd edition). Mahwah, NJ: Lawrence Erlbaum Associates.

Hiley, J. (2010). *The current mentorship model is broken. Retrieved January 24, 2013 from http://www.articlesbase.com/ college-and-university-articles/the-current-mentorship-model-is-broken-1875434.html*

Hilliard, A. G. (1995). *The maroon within us: Selected essays on African American community socializations.* Baltimore, MD: Black Classic Press.

Hodgetts, K. (September, 2008). Underperformance or "getting it right"? Constructions of gender and achievement in the Australian inquiry into boys' education. *British Journal of Sociology of Education, 29*(5), 465–477.

Honora, D. T. (Summer, 2002). The relationship of gender and achievement to future outlook among African American adolescents. *Adolescence, 37*(146), 301-316.

Honora, D. T. (January, 2003). Urban African American adolescents and school identification. *Urban Education, 38*(1), 58-76.

Chapter III: The Art of Being Cool

Jackson, C., & Dempster, S. (December, 2009). "I sat back on my computer . . . with a bottle of whisky next to me": Constructing "cool" masculinity through "effortless" achievement in secondary and higher education. *Journal of Gender Studies, 18*(4), 341–356.

Janzen, J. M. (October, 1972). Laman's Kongo ethnography: Observations on sources, methodology and theory. *Africa, 42*(4), 316-328.

Jekielek, S. M., Moore, K. A., & Hair, E. C. (2002). *Mentoring programs and youth development: A synthesis.* Washington, DC: Child Trends and Edna McConnell Clark Foundation.

Jung, C. G. (1966). *The spirit in man, art, and literature.* New York: Pantheon.

Jung, C. G., et al. (Eds.). (1964). *Man and his symbols.* New York: Anchor Books Doubleday.

Kunjufu, J. (1988). *To be popular or smart: The Black peer group.* Chicago: African American Images.

Kuzmic, J. J. (2000). Textbooks, knowledge, and masculinity: Examining patriarchy from within. In N. Lesko (Ed.), *Masculinities at school* (pp. 105-126). Thousand Oaks, CA: Sage.

Lee, C. D. (2000). Signifying in the zone of proximal development. In C. D. Lee & P. Smatorinsky (Eds.), *Vygotskian perspectives on literacy research.* New York: Cambridge University Press.

Leland, J. (2004). *Hip: The history.* New York: HarperCollins.

Lewis, S., et al. (2010). *A call for change: The social and educational factors contributing to the outcomes of Black males in urban schools.* Washington, DC: The Council of the Great City Schools.

Majors, R., & Billson, J. M. (1993). *Cool pose: The dilemmas of Black manhood in America.* New York: Simon and Schuster.

Martin, A., et al. (2003). Self-handicapping and defensive pessimism: A model of self-protection from a longitudinal perspective. *Contemporary Educational Psychology, 28*(1), 1–36.

Martino, W., & Pallotta-Chiarolli, M. (2003). *So what's a boy? Addressing issues of masculinity and schooling*. Philadelphia, PA: Open University Press.

Martino, W., & Kehler, M. D. (2007). Gender-based literacy reform: A question of challenging or recuperating gender binaries. *Canadian Journal of Education*. Special Issue. M. Kehler & W. Martino (Guest Editors). *Boys, Literacy and Schooling, 30*(2), 406-431.

Marx, K. (1971). Preface. *A contribution to the critique of political economy,* Trans. S. W. Ryanzanskaya, M. Dobb (Ed.). London: Lawrence & Whishart.

McGrath, D., & Van Buskirk, B. (1996). Social and emotional capital in education: Cultures of support for at risk students. *Journal of Developmental Education, 1*(1).

McKenry, P., Everett, J., Ramseur, H., & Carter, C. (1989). Research on Black adolescents: A legacy of cultural bias. *Journal of Adolescent Research, 4*(2), 254-264.

Millard, E. (1997). *Differently literate: Boys, girls and the schooling of literacy*. London: Falmer Press.

Miller, N. E., & Dollard, J. (1941). *Social learning and imitation*. New Haven: Yale University Press.

Moses, R. P., & Cobb, C. E. (2001). *Radical equations: Math, literacy, and civil rights*. Boston: Beacon Press.

Myers, W. D. (2001). *Monster*. New York: Amistad.

Myers, W. D. (2002). *Bad boy: A memoir*. New York: Amistad.

National Urban League. (1992). *Mentoring young Black males: An overview*. New York: National Urban League, Youth Services.

Neal, L., et al. (Spring, 2003). The effects of African American movement styles on teachers' perceptions and reactions. *Journal of Special Education, 37*(1), 49-57.

Newman, N. (2010). Machismo: A cultural barrier to learning. *Young Latino males: An American dilemma*. Retrieved April 2, 2012 from http://cronkitezine.asu.edu/latinomales/machismo.html

Chapter III: The Art of Being Cool

Organization of Economic Cooperation and Development (OECD). (2006). *Education at a glance.* Retrieved January 3, 2013 from http://www.oecd.org/edu/skills-beyond-school/educationataglance2006-home.htm

Ogbu, J. (2008). *Minority status, oppositional culture, & schooling.* New York: Routledge.

O'Sullivan, A., & Sheffrin, S. (2003). *Economics: Principles in action.* Needham, MA: Prentice Hall.

Padilla, A. M. (2004). Quantitative methods in multicultural education research. In J. Banks & C. Banks (Eds.), *Handbook of research in multicultural education (2nd ed.).* San Francisco: Jossey-Bass.

Portes, A. (1998). Social capital: its origins and applications in modern sociology. *Annual Review of Sociology, 24,* 1–24.

Reay, D. (2004). Cultural capitalists and academic habitus: classed and gendered labor in UK higher education. *Women's Studies International Forum, 27*(1), 31–39.

Roediger, D. R. (2005). *Working toward whiteness: How America's immigrants became white: The strange journey from Ellis Island to the suburbs.* New York: Basic Books.

Saville-Troike, M. (1989). *The ethnography of communication.* New York: Basil Blackwell.

Slavin, R., & Oickle, E. (1981). Effects of cooperative learning teams on student achievement and race relations: Treatment by race interactions. *Sociology of Education, 54*(3), 174-180.

Shade, B. J., Kelly, C. A., & Oberg, M. (1997). *Creating culturally responsive classrooms.* Washington, DC: American Psychological Association.

Simpson, A. (December, 1996). Fictions and facts: An investigation of the reading practices of girls and boys. *English Education, 28*(4), 268-279.

Steinberg, L. (1993). *Adolescence* (3rd ed.). New York: McGraw-Hill.

Stevens, L. P., & Bean, T. W. (2007). *Critical literacy: Context, research and practice in the K-12 classroom*. Thousand Oaks, CA: Sage.

Tatum, A. W. (Spring, 2008). Toward a more anatomically complete model of literacy instruction: A focus on African male adolescents and texts. *Harvard Educational Review, 78*(1), 155-180.

Taylor-Butler, C., & Page, M. (2003). *No boys allowed!* New York: Scholastic.

Thompson, R. F. (1984). *Flash of the spirit: African & Afro-American art & philosophy*. New York: Random House.

Torrance, E. P. (1984). *Mentoring relationships: How they aid creative achievement, endure, change, and die*. Buffalo, NY: Bearly.

Treffinger, D. J. (2003). The role of mentoring in talent development. In K. W. McCluskey & A. Mays (Eds.), *Mentoring for talent development* (pp. 1-11). Sioux Falls, SD: Reclaiming Youth International.

Trivani Foundation. (March, 2009). Literacy in the United States. *Trivani Foundation Newsletter: Family Literacy Centers*. Retrieved October 2, 2010 from http://www. wrenchproject .com/linked/family literacy centers.pdf

Trueba, H. T. (1993). Castification in multicultural America. In H. Trueba, C. Rodriguez, Y.

Zou, & J. Cintron (Eds.), *Healing multicultural America: Mexican immigrants rise to power in rural California* (pp. 29-51). Washington, DC: Falmer Press.

Valdes, G. (1996). *Con respecto: Bridging the distance between culturally diverse families and schools*. New York: Teachers College Press.

Weaver-Hightower, M. (2003). The "boy turn" in research on gender and education. *Review of Educational Research, 73*(4), 471-498

Wedgwood, N. (2009). Connell's theory of masculinity—its origins and influences on the study of gender. *Journal of Gender Studies, 18*(4), 329-339.

Chapter III: The Art of Being Cool

Wilkins, A. C. (2008). *Wannabes, goths, and Christians: The boundaries of sex, style and status.* Chicago: University of Chicago Press.

Younger, M., & Warrington, M. (2005). *Raising boys' achievement in secondary schools.* Maidenhead, NY: Open University Press.

Zipp, G. P., & Olson, V. (September, 2008). Infusing the mentorship model of education for the promotion of critical thinking in doctoral education. *Journal of College Teacher & Learning, 5*(9), 9-16.

Chapter IV: Black Males and the School-to-Prison Pipeline

My people are destroyed from lack of knowledge.

Hosea 4:6

Every time you stop a school,

you will have to build a jail.

Mark Twain,

Mark Twain Quotes, 1900

The Art of Being Cool

Introduction

A few years ago, I was sitting in a black barbershop waiting for a haircut. Black barbershops historically have reputations as places where conversations are lively, entertaining, and informative. Barbershops are one of the places where Black men gather together not only to be groomed to look cool, but to learn social trends and glean information on what others may think is cool as well. A Black barbershop is one of the few places that African American men from various religions, different social economic statuses and varying ages regularly meet. I had one such conversation with a man sitting in a chair across from me. We exchanged pleasantries and he asked me what I did for a living. At the time, I was considering whether to apply right away for PhD programs after I finished my master's degree or whether to spend some time visiting and conducting research in Africa. He told me that if I wanted to understand Black people I should do research in U.S. prisons. The implication is that with so many Black men in prison this should be the place to start research.

In fact, prison culture is so predominant in the Black community that many males see prison as a rite of passage or something that is cool. My response was, "Did you just tell a Black man that he should go to prison instead of getting a PhD?" He said that his point was the oppression of Black people in the U.S. in the past is the same as it is today with the exception that prisons have taken the place of slave ships and prison labor is the modern day form of slavery. This may lead some people to wonder, "Since slavery was a long time ago and we have moved on from there, why should we care any longer that it happened at all?" (Gillborn, 2006) Others might ask, "What does prison have to do with slavery?"

This brief literature review will attempt to answer those questions. The evidence is clear: The U.S. education system and the juvenile justice system have created a school-to-prison-to-incarceration-to-enslavement-to-forced labor pipeline that is indeed a modern form of slavery.

Purpose. The purpose of this chapter is to examine the school-to-prison pipeline structure by first establishing a historical foundation and then moving to a brief analysis of preventive programs that can help dismantle it. To that end, this chapter begins with the historical foundations of education and incarceration in the U.S., and follows with a section on methodology to provide a theoretical and conceptual framework. The next section provides an analysis that traces the school-to-prison-to-enslavement-to-forced labor pipeline that flows from the education system, to the juvenile justice system, to the prison industrial complex and results in the prison system functioning as a modern day plantation. It concludes with a sample of cost-effective, preventive programs and recommendations for dismantling the school-to-prison-to-enslavement-to-forced labor pipeline.

Historical Foundations of Education and Incarceration in the U.S.

There is a history of denying education to and incarceration of Blacks in the United States. For example, in 1827, Frederick Douglass heard his owner scold his wife and reprimand her for teaching him how to read the Bible. As Douglass (1845) recounts in his *Narrative,* "'If you teach that n***** how to read, there would be no keeping him'" and he would "'become unmanageable, and of no value to his master'" (p. 33). While the incident of 1827 involved just a verbal punishment, by 1831, a bill was passed preventing slaves from learning how to read and write, and was later enforced by imprisonment. Prudence Crandall was placed in jail for educating Blacks in 1834; Mrs. Margaret Douglass of Norfolk, Virginia, was placed in prison for teaching Blacks to read in 1853 (North Carolina Digital History, 2010). Even if a formerly enslaved person escaped bondage and found freedom, the person was still under constant surveillance. The United States Congress passed fugitive slave laws in 1793, legalizing the return of slaves to their owners even if they had escaped to free states.

The right to educate Black Americans was officially denied in the 1857 *Dred Scott v. Sandford* court case. More commonly known as the Dred Scott Decision, this U.S. Supreme Court case ruled that people of African descent imported as slaves and their descendants—free or not—were not considered citizens of the United States. This held force until the Emancipation Proclamation in 1863. The U.S. Constitution's Thirteenth Amendment, Section 1 states, "Neither slavery nor involuntary servitude, *except as a punishment for crime whereof the party shall have been duly convicted,* shall exist within the United States" (emphasis added, Legal Information Institute, 2010). This amendment made it legal to rent prisoners and pay wages directly to sheriffs and judges (Franklin, 2000). Using this loophole in the law allowed those who were imprisoned before emancipation and those who were imprisoned after emancipation (sometimes falsely convicted) to be used as slave labor. Many former slaveholders and plantation landowners became prison guards (Schenwar, 2008).

Many laws were created that made it legal to separate those who had been enslaved and those who were not. The Jim Crow laws administered between 1876 and 1965 enforced racial separation between Whites and Blacks, including schools that were authorized by state and local governments. Jim Crow laws made disbursement of substandard education due to racial prejudice easily concealable. In 1896, the *Plessy v. Ferguson* case made racial separation illegal. Nevertheless, it was not until 1954 that the *Brown v. Board of Education of Topeka* case ruled that separate but unequal education of Black and White children was unconstitutional. However, while not officially legal, education in the U.S. is still unofficially separate and unequal. The minoritized suffer at an immensely disproportionate rate in regards to education, which makes the equalizing of the education system for every U.S. citizen one of the largest social justice questions of our time (*Las Vegas Sentinel Voice*, 2010; Legend, 2010). In fact, scholars, educators, and lawyers have come up with a special lens with which to examine issues related to class, ethnicity, and race.

Theoretical Framework

This chapter employs the theoretical framework of critical race theory (CRT). CRT originally emerged from post-civil rights legal issues. Currently, CRT is also employed by educators as a framework in which to apply issues related to both the educational system and the juvenile justice system. CRT is an analytical framework that focuses on history, economics, equity, constitutional law, and of course racism (Delgado & Stefancic, 2001). Since race is a social construct, a theory that has social implications has value for understanding the social dynamics behind school dropouts and suspension as well as prison incarcerations.

Literature

We are building more prisons than ever before and school dropout rates are increasing. Classrooms are overcrowded, and to fix the problem, classrooms are filled with undertrained and overworked teachers. The few effective teachers are undervalued and underpaid (Mendez, 2003). Current teacher attrition rates indicate that half quit the profession in five years (Lambert, 2006). Additionally, as a result of or as a culmination of these problems, schools in the U.S. are unfairly placing students in detention or suspending them outright. Once a student has a juvenile record of suspension, the student's likelihood of graduating on time decreases and the circumstances that lead to prison incarceration increase (Mendez, 2003). Once individuals are placed in prison, in addition to incarceration hardships, inmates also suffer from exploitation. Prisons inmates manufacture various products from circuit boards to lingerie (Evans & Goldberg, 1997). This school-to-prison-to-enslavement-to-forced labor pipeline affects minoritized students and students with low social economic status (SES) and perpetuates a vicious cycle of exploitation. In essence, if you are a minoritized student or attend a school in a poor neighborhood, you are more likely to wind up in prison than your non-minority, upper-income peers.

Chapter IV: Black Males and the School-to-Prison Pipeline

Analysis

The Education System

America's cumulative effects of racial inequity are causing both an academic crisis and an incarceration crisis. We are imprisoning more people in the United States than ever before. In fact, the U.S. incarcerates more people than any other country in the world (Warren, Gelb, Horowitz, & Riordan, 2009). The minoritized make up a substantial portion of this large sample of incarcerated Americans, 1 in 100 (Warren, et al., 2009). Many of those incarcerated are dropouts.

At first glance, it appears the nation's prison population voluntarily chose to drop out since most of them have not completed high school. The truth is that incarceration often precedes dropping out of school (Coalition for Juvenile Justice, 2001). In fact, unqualified teachers, lack of resources, and even fewer opportunities to take college preparatory classes often push students, especially minoritized students and students from lower SES, out of school (U.S. Department of Education, 2001). Additionally, the United States is spending less money on schools and more money on prisons (Warren, et al., 2009). These same students suffer from inattentive and overworked teachers, are often tested on material they never reviewed, and are more likely to be held back or suspended than their White counterparts (Mendez, 2003). State spending from corrections institutions increased at six times the spending rate on higher education between 1980 and 2000 (Wald & Losen, 2003). Although Black students made up only 17% of the overall population in 2000, they made up 34% of all suspensions (U.S. Department of Education, 2001). What is even more troubling is that fewer than 95% of juvenile court cases involved a violent offense (Public Citizens for Children and Youth, 2000). Additionally, U.S. schools' suspensions have almost doubled in the last 30 years (Smollin, 2010).

The number of suspensions that a sixth-grade student receives has a strong positive relationship to suspensions in seventh and eighth grades and a negative relationship to on-time graduation rates (Wald & Losen, 2003). Difficulty being readmitted into the school system after suspension or expulsion is a large component of the school-to-prison path and subsequent incarceration-to-enslavement-to-forced labor pipeline. Not only are students marked as potential troublemakers after a suspension or expulsion, it is not uncommon for students to be targeted and placed on high surveillance by both truant officers and school-assigned police officers (Golden, Suegel, & Forsythe, 2010). Unfortunately, aggressive enforcement policies like zero-tolerance lead to increases of suspensions and expulsions, and too many suspensions and expulsions often lead to incarceration. Less than 15% of students who return to the public school system after an incarceration graduate (Balfanz, et al., 2003). Additionally, students who return to school from suspension or expulsion often have fallen behind due to missed class time.

The more time students spend out of school, the less time they have received educational instruction and access to school materials. "The link between illiteracy and incarceration rates is so strong that some states decide the number of prison cells to build based on fourth grade reading levels" (Trivani, 2009). In one study, two-thirds of incarcerated male students had been suspended one or more times by eighth grade (Balfanz, et al., 2003). Only 15% of students who repeat the ninth grade complete their secondary education (Balfanz, et al.). "Seventy-five percent of youth under the age of eighteen who were sentenced to adult prisons have not passed tenth grade" (Wald & Losen, 2003, p. 11). Clearly, there is a pattern of the U.S. educational system feeding students to the juvenile justice system in a school-to-prison pipeline that ends in incarceration, enslavement, and forced labor.

The Juvenile Justice System

America is having a juvenile justice problem, and this phenomenon is especially troubling for people of color. For example, school suspension rates are higher for the minoritized in the U.S. (Mendez, 2003). The cause for the increase in school suspensions has been associated with recent zero-tolerance policies. Zero-tolerance policies include predetermined consequences despite the severity of the infraction (Wald & Losen, 2003). Not only are African American students more likely to be formally charged once they are sent to juvenile court because of aggressively applied zero-tolerance policies, they are also more likely to be waived over to adult court (National Council on Crime and Delinquency, 2007). In fact, since 45 states have passed laws making it easier to try juveniles as adults, minorities are affected most (Mendez, 2003).

While it is not reasonable to think that all suspensions or incarcerations of minorities are entirely unwarranted, it stands to reason racial differences play some role in incarcerations (Lorde, 1984). Pope, Lovell, and Hsia (2002) contend that race plays a role in one stage or another of the juvenile justice process with a cumulative effect. This cumulative effect is based on racial disadvantages that influence a series of decisions: to make the initial arrest, hold a youth in detention pending investigation, refer a case to juvenile court, waive a case to adult court, petition a case for prosecution, and rule, as a judge would and subsequently apply sanctions (National Council on Crime and Delinquency, 2007).

This cumulative effect has residual results outside of juvenile court. It is reflected in the high accusation rate and conviction rate of young Black men combined with a Black male imprisonment rate that is seven times higher than White males between the ages of 20 and 39 in the U.S. (Dyson, 2007). However, cumulative effects have compounded for African American males who suffer from lack of educational equity, employment, and underemployment. Du Bois eventually came to believe the nation's superstructure would not spend more money for educational institutions that empower former slaves and provide opportunities that would enable them to effectively compete with Whites (Johnson, 1976). In fact, the only time a Black male applicant is considered equal to a White male applicant is when the White male has a criminal record or is incarcerated (Pager, 2003). Put simply, African American males are powerless inside and outside of the prison infrastructure. From this lens, "power is not an institution, and not a structure; neither is it a certain strength we are endowed with; it is the name that one attributes to a complex strategical situation in a particular society" (Foucault, 1998, p. 93).

Plea Bargaining

As described earlier, a great many of the inmates in prisons are placed there as a result of circumstances related to being suspended in school. This occurs despite the fact that out-of-school suspension seldom deters inappropriate behavior and does not increase school safety (Mendez, 2003). Zero-tolerance policies that lead to suspensions typically lead to probation. In fact, many states incarcerate students or place them on probation after three or more suspensions. As of 2004, there were four million Americans on probation (Bikel, 2004). Many of them have been on probation for minor offenses such as truancy and petty theft under 100 dollars. To unburden the court system, those accused of minor crimes are often encouraged to plea to a lesser charge. Ninety-five percent of felony convictions never reach trial because of plea bargains (Bikel). Unfortunately, due to lack of knowledge about the justice system, many Americans who plea to a lesser charge often wind up worse off. For example, if you miss a probation payment or restitution payment that was part of a plea bargain you can wind up in jail. In some cases, if you do not take a plea and cannot afford bail you can spend five months in prison (Bikel). Once a person receives a prison sentence it increases the chances of that person becoming a repeat offender and being exploited while in prison. This is clear evidence that the prison industry is a powerful device which oppresses physically, emotionally, and financially.

The Prison Industry

Prisons do not have to pay inmates. This makes hiring workers who are incarcerated particularly desirable. This is not only about hiring prisoners, though. The prison industry is one of the largest growing, most lucrative industries in the U.S. (Pelaez, 2008). For example, in California, many public schools and universities are provided with furniture manufactured by prison inmates (Davis, 2003). Massingill and Sohn assert that revenue from local prisons supports many small towns in Texas (2007). In just one example, Texas offered "rent-a-cell" services to other states that had overcrowded prisons. "Rent-a-cell" salespeople earn a commission of $2.50 to $5.50 per day and bed, and the local county that houses the inmates earns $1.50 for each prisoner (Pelaez, 2008). Southern states like Texas account for four out of every 10 people incarcerated in the U.S. and one out of every 11 incarcerated in the world (Rachel & Burch, 2003). Due to numbers like these, the prison industrial complex is not only lucrative, but also sustainable.

One Texas prison is almost entirely self-sustainable. Prisoners manufacture the razor wire on the fences surrounding the prison; they also manufacture the janitorial supplies; they grow the cotton, and weave it into the fabrics used for prison uniforms, towels, and blankets; they even manufacture the toothpaste they use. Additionally, prisoners build the prison cells. Money to invest in prison construction has come from some of the largest companies in the U.S., such as Merrill-Lynch, Shearson-Lehman, American Express, and Allstate (Palaez, 2008). Inmates perform data entry for TWA, raise hogs, make circuit boards, limousines, water beds, lingerie (Evans & Goldberg, 1997), and correctional officers' uniforms (Massingill & Sohn, 2008). Money that is circulated within the prison industry from tax revenue as well as grants and profits is not usually shared with inmates. Products manufactured in prison and sold outside prisons pay inmates below minimum wage or not at all. When prisons do decide to pay, the wages are so low it is akin to modern day slavery.

Prisons: Modern Plantations

From 1972 to 1975, Angola Prison in Louisiana paid its inmates 4 cents per hour (Schenwar, 2008). Today in Louisiana, prisoners' workweek hours have been reduced from 96 hours to 40 hours, and wages have been increased to 40 cents an hour (Glasser, 2010). However, prison income is held until inmates are released (Schenwar,

Chapter IV: Black Males and the School-to-Prison Pipeline

2008). This does little good if prisoners are sentenced to life. Extra work hours can also be given as a form of punishment.

Common crops for prison farmland are soybean, corn, wheat, and cotton (Glasser, 2010). It is not uncommon for prisons in the South to enforce mandatory farm labor among its prisoners. The incentive for cheap labor may be why the South has incarcerated four out of 10 imprisoned people in the U.S. and one out of every 11 prisoners in the world (Herzing & Burch, 2003). Southern states like Arkansas have mandatory farm labor for 40% of its inmates; in Texas, the figure is 17% of its inmates and in Louisiana 16% of its inmates have mandatory farm labor.

A large part of the land that former slave owners held in Alabama, Arkansas, Mississippi, Tennessee, Texas, and Louisiana was sold and used to build prisons. Described by Van Jones as "slave ships on dry land" (Jones, 2007; Reiland, 2009), this is the land to which enslaved people came to America on ships as captives and were forced to plant, pick, and harvest crops. This has become the land on which crops are planted, picked, and harvested by enslaved prison inmates who are now incarcerated captives. Many prison guards in the South are descendants of former slave owners and plantation overseers (Schenwar, 2008). This is the final component in the school-to-prison-to-incarceration-to-enslavement-to-forced labor pipeline.

Conclusions

If the U.S. does not do something to prevent this pipeline and subsequent entrenchment of inmate/slave labor, we will not only lose millions of students to poverty and despair, we will lose the potential to empower an entire generation to improve the world. Clearly, we need a new strategy to address this problem. Just showing a little care goes a long way with students (Wald & Losen, 2003). After-school initiatives and preventive programs may be a solution to stem this epidemic and the cultural association with prison as not merely an inevitability, but something that young people can perceive as cool.

Recommendations

Preventive Programs

Not all such programs are effective. For example, *Scared Straight* programs and boot camps all have a cost-to-benefit loss of $24,531 and $3,587 per student respectively; in addition, *DARE* is ineffective (Osher, Quinn, Poirier, & Rutherford, 2003). Additionally, although

The Art of Being Cool

the *Boys and Girls Clubs of America (BGCA)* have been shown to foster academic achievement in some cities, they have also been shown to increase substance abuse (Anderson-Butcher, Newsome, & Ferrari 2003). Although not all preventive programs are effective, some are more effective and cost efficient than others.

Some preventive programs do work. Osher, Quinn, Poirier, & Rutherford (2003) did a cost-benefits review of effective programs. *Nurse-Family Partnership*, an intervention where home health care nurses make weekly home visits to at-risk, low-income, and first-time pregnant women reap benefits of $2 for every $1 invested. The *Perry Preschool Program* that targets social, intellectual, and physical development of children living in poverty through weekly home visits has had positive results with an estimated cost-to-benefit ratio of $10 for every $7.16 spent. *The Seattle Social Development Project* increases opportunities for active involvement in family and school life as well as school and peer groups and provides positive recognition for young people. It has an estimated cost-to-benefit ratio of $3 for every $1 spent. This is achieved through workshops and classroom coaching for teachers, parenting workshops, and social and citizenship training skills. *Aggression Replacement Therapy*, combating learned aggressive behavior with other solutions has an estimated cost-benefit ratio of $45 for every $1 spent. *Wraparound*, a child- and family-driven planning process that provides services rather than penalties, has a reduction of recidivism by half. *Multisystemic Therapy* offers approaches that are provided in the home and it has an estimated $28 return for every $1 invested. *The Functional Family Therapy*, an intervention strategy that reduces conduct disorder, delinquency, substance abuse, and family conflict for youths ages 11 to 18 who are at risk, provides engagement motivation, behavior change, and prevention of recurring delinquent behavior. It has an estimated cost-to-benefit ratio of $27 for every $1 spent. *Multidimensional Treatment Foster Care,* where families with no more than two children are recruited, trained, and supported, has an estimated cost-to-benefit ratio of $43 for every $1 spent.

Kentucky Jefferson County Public Schools (JCPS) in collaboration with the Louisville Urban League has sponsored the preventive program *The Street Academy. The Street Academy* is a 22-week pilot program targeting 40 male fourth, fifth, and sixth graders who have been classified as novice readers. The cost per student is approximately $1000. All of the students attend Title I schools. The Saturday-school program is based on the National Urban League's *Street Academies* in New York City and the *Piney Woods Academy* in Mississippi and includes martial arts training, literacy, and math. While actual cost-to-benefit ratio was not reported, a correlation between low literacy rates and below grade level reading and math performance was associated with poor eyesight (Glewwe, Park, & Zhao, 2000). Since the majority of the children in the *Street Academy* are from low SES, this finding suggests that providing eye exams and eyeglasses are effective components to increasing education outcomes.

Additionally, *Early Childhood* programs have been proven to be effective with a positive estimated cost-benefit ratio of $7.10 for every $1 spent (Coalition for Juvenile Justice, 2001). For severely disadvantaged children, participation in *pre-kindergarten* has been found to significantly reduce both juvenile and adult crime, increase high school graduation rates, and improve employment opportunities and earnings, with an estimated cost-to-benefit ratio of $16 for every $1 spent (Schweinhart, et al., 2005). *The STAR (Student Teacher Achievement Ratio) Project* in Tennessee showed that students randomly assigned to smaller classes of between 13 to 17 students in grades K-3 outperformed their peers in regular or regular-plus-aide classes of between 22 to 25 students (Hagopian, 2009). Finally, establishing a clear goal, using data to measure progress, adapting strategies when necessary, and being relentless in the pursuit of objectives have proven to be effective means of changing political will (Osher, et al., 2003).

To be fair, not all schools are part of the school-to-prison-to-forced labor pipeline. However, to dismantle the ones that are seems to require programs like the above that nurture and support students in culturally responsible ways. These programs seem to provide the most cost-effective solutions to prevent the school-to-prison-to-incarceration-to-forced labor pipeline. Additionally, when it comes to positive outcomes and after-school or intervention programs, it is the administrators and the teachers that make the difference, no matter what the cost-to-benefit ratio of a program happens to achieve. Support from school personnel is a far greater indicator of parental response to school involvement than SES or ethnicity (Harry & Klingner, 2006).

My recommendation is to further study each of the programs individually and create new models based on these programs' proven track records. For example, in California it costs more to incarcerate a felon than it does to send two students to a flagship university such as the University of California, three students to California State, or seven students to California Community College (Davidson, 1997). Do you know the price in 2002 of one year's incarceration in Nevada? One thousand, six hundred, and fourteen dollars (Western Interstate Commission for Higher Education, 2002). What was the price in 2002 of a year of college at the University of Nevada, Reno? Nine thousand, four hundred and forty-two dollars (Western Interstate Commission for Higher Education, 2002). Can you tell me the price of an after-school program in Las Vegas? *Priceless*. The cost of an after-school program far outweighs the alternative. It may very well be that the right intervention program or a combination of the programs listed above will result in a juvenile minority going to a flagship school such as Princeton University instead heading to prison.

Chapter IV: Black Males and the School-to-Prison Pipeline

References

Anderson-Butcher, D., Newsome, W., & Ferrari, T. (2003). Participation in Boys and Girls Clubs and relationships to youth outcomes. *Journal of Community Psychology, 31*(1), 39-55.

Balfanz, R., Spiridakis, K., Neild, R., & Legters, N. (2003). *High poverty secondary schools and the juvenile justice system: how neither helps the other and how that could change.* Paper presented at School to Prison Pipeline Conference, Harvard Civil Rights Project, Cambridge, MA. Available at http://www.csos.jhu.edu/crespar/tech Reports/Report70.pdf

Banks, J. (2006). Democracy, diversity, and social justice: Educating citizens for the public interest in a global age. In Gloria Ladson-Billings and William Tate (Eds.), *Education Research in the Public Interest: Social Justice, Action, and Policy.* Multicultural Education Series. New York: Teachers College Press.

Bikel, O. (Director), & Lyman, W. (Actor), (2004). *The plea.* Virginia: Melbourne, PBS Video. Coalition for Juvenile Justice.

Coalition for Juvenile Justice. (2001). *Abandoned in the back row: New lessons in education and delinquency prevention.* Washington, DC: Author.

Davidson, J. (October, 1997). Caged cargo: African Americans are grist for the fast-growing prison industry's money mill. *Emerge*, 36-46.

Davis, A. Y. (2003). *Are prisons obsolete?* New York: Seven Stories Press.

Delgado, R., & Stefancic, J. (2001). *Critical race theory: An introduction.* New York: New York University Press.

Douglass, F. (1845). *Narrative of the life of Frederick Douglass.* Boston: Anti-Slavery Office.

Dyson, M. (2007). *Debating race with Michael Eric Dyson.* New York: Basic Civitas Books.

Evans L., & Goldberg, E. (1997). *The prison industrial complex and the global economy.* Berkeley, CA: Prison Activist Resource Center.

Foucault, M. (1998). *The history of sexuality. Vol. 1: The will to knowledge.* London: Penguin.

Franklin, H. B. (December, 2000). *From Plantation to Penitentiary to the Prison-Industrial Complex: Literature of the American Prison.* Paper delivered at the Modern Language Association Convention.

Gillborn, D. (2006). Public interest and the interests of White people are not the same: Assessment, education policy and racism. In G. Ladson-Billings & W. Tate (Eds.), *Education research in the public interest: Social justice, action, and policy.* Multicultural Education Series. New York: Teachers College Press.

Glasser, I. (December 25, 2008,). Christmas Day in a Louisiana dungeon. *The Huffington Post.* http://www.huffington post. com/ira-glasser/christmas-day-in-a-louisi_b_153349.html

Glewwe, P., Park, A., & Zhao, M. (2000). The Ganshu Vision Intervention Project. http://reap.standford.edu Golden, M., Suegel, V., & Forsythe, D. (2010). Approaches to school safety in America's largest cities. *Vera Institute of Justice.* Retrieved September 27, 2010 from http://www.vera .org/content/approaches-school-safety-americas-largest-cities

Hagopian, J. (2009). The dog eats its tail: Oversized classes, over-populated prisons. *Common Dreams.* Retrieved September 27, 2010 from http://www.common dreams.org/view/2009/ 03/07-2

Harry, B., & Klingner, J. (2006). *Why are so many minority students in special education? Understanding race and disability in schools.* New York: Teachers College Press.

Herzing, R., & Burch, M. (November, 2003). Challenging the prison industrial complex. *USA Today: Society for the*

Advancement of Education. Retrieved October 5, 2010 from http://find articles.com/p/articles/mi_m1272/is_2702_132/ai_110531025/

Johnson, A. (1976). *A history and interpretation of the William Edward Burghardt Du Bois-Booker Talliaferro Washington higher educational controversy*. Los Angeles: University of Southern California.

Jones, V. (January, 2007). Van Jones at the National Conference for Media Reform. Memphis, TN: NCMR and Free Press. Uploaded January 6, 2007. http://www.youtube.com/watch?v=n2z6n000-2Y

Lambert, L. (May, 2006). Half of teachers quit in five years: Working conditions, low salaries cited. *Washington Post*. Retrieved October 3, 2010 from http://www.washingtonpost.com/wpdyn/content/article/2006/05/08/AR2006050801344.html

Las Vegas Sentinel Voice. (November 11, 2010). Colleges more diverse, but racial gaps exist. *Las Vegas Sentinel-Voice*.

Legal Information Institute. (2010). *United States Constitution, Amendment XIII*. Cornell University Law School. Retrieved October 5, 2010 from http://topics.law.cornell.edu/constitution/amendmentxiii

Legend, J. (January, 2010). Education reform: The civil rights issue of our time. *The Huffington Post*. Retrieved November 14, 2010 from http://www.huffington post.com/john-legend/education-reform-the-civi_b_426490.html

Lorde, A. (1984). *Sister outsider*. Freedom, CA: The Crossing Press.

Massingill, R., & Sohn, A. B. (2007). *Prison city: Life with the death penalty in Huntsville, Texas*. New York: Peter Lang Publishing.

Mendez, L. M. (2003). Predictors of suspension and negative school outcomes: A longitudinal investigation. In J. Wald & D. Losen (Eds.), *Deconstructing the school-to-prison pipeline: New directions for youth development (Number 99)*. San Francisco: Jossey-Bass.

National Council on Crime and Delinquency. (January, 2007). *And justice for some: Differential treatment of youth of color in the justice system.* Retrieved October 22, 2012 from http://www.nccdglobal.org/sites/default/files/publication_pdf/justice-for-some.pdf

North Carolina Digital History (2010). *A bill to prevent all persons from teaching slaves to read or write, the use of figures accepted (1830).* Legislative Papers, 1830–31, Session of the General Assembly. Retrieved from http://www.learnnc.org/lp/editions/nchist-newnation/4384

Osher, D., Quinn, M., Poirier, J., & Rutherford, R. (2003). Deconstructing the pipeline: Using efficacy, effectiveness, and cost-benefit data to reduce minority youth incarceration. *New Directions for Youth Development, 99,* 91-120.

Pager, D. (2003).The mark of a criminal record. *American Journal of Sociology, 108,* 937-975.

Papa, A. (August, 23, 2010). An end to prison gerrymandering. *New York Times.* http://www.nytimes.com/2010/08/23/opinion/23mon3.html?_r=o

Pelaez, V. (2008). The *prison industry in the United States: Big business or a new form of slavery?* Retrieved October 3, 2010 from http://www.globalresearch.ca/index.php? context=va&aid=8289

Pope, C. E., Lovell, R., & Hsia, H. M. (2002). *Disproportionate Minority Confinement: A Review of the Research Literature from 1989 through 2001.* Washington, DC: Office of Juvenile Justice and Delinquency Prevention. Accessed October 24, 2006 from http://ojjdp.ncjrs.org/dmc/pdf/dmc89_01.pdf

Price, B. (September 13, 2010). Pathways to prison and poverty. *The Atlanta Post.* Retrieved September 27, 2012 from http://atlantapost.com/2010/09/13/pathways-to-prison-and-poverty/

Public Citizens for Children and Youth (PCCY). (2000). *Court watch 1999-2000.* Available at http://www.pccy.org/PDF/courtwatch2000/pdf

Reiland, R. (2009). Van's line. *The New Spectator.* Retrieved October 4, 2010 from http://www.thenewspectator.org/archives/2009/09/17/vans-line

Schenwar, M. (2008). *Slavery haunts America's plantation prisons.* Retrieved October 4, 2010 from http://realcost of prisons.org/ blog/archives/2008/09/slavery_haunts.html

Schweinhart, L. J., Montie, J., Xiang, Z., Barnett, W. S., Belfield, C. R., & Nores, M. (2005). *Lifetime effects: The high/ scope Perry preschool study through age 40.* (Monographs of The High/Scope Educational Research Foundation, 14). Ypsilanti, MI: High/Scope Press.

Smollin, M. (2010). Zero tolerance almost doubles school suspensions. *Take part: Inspiration to action.* Retrieved October 30, 2010 from http://www.takepart .com/news/ 2010/09/22/zero-tolerancealmost-doubles-school-suspensions

Trivani Foundation. (2009). *Trivani Foundation Newsletter: Family Literacy Centers.* Retrieved October 2, 2010 from http://www.trivanifoundation.org/news/marnewsletter 09.pdf

Twain, M. (1900). *Mark Twain quotes.* Retrieved October 30, 2010 from http://www.twainquotes.com/School.html

U.S. Department of Education. Office of Civil Rights. (2001). *Elementary and secondary school survey: National and state projections.* Washington, DC: U.S. Government Printing Office.

Wald, J., & Kurlaender, M. (2003). Connected in Seattle? An exploratory study of student perceptions of discipline and attachment to others. In J. Wald & D. Losen (Eds.), *Deconstructing the school-to-prison pipeline: New directions for youth development (Number 99).* San Francisco: Jossey-Bass.

Wald, J. & Losen, D. (2003). Defining and redirecting a school-to-prison pipeline. In J. Wald & D. Losen (Eds.), *Deconstructing the school-to-prison pipeline: New directions for youth development (Number 99).* San Francisco: Jossey-Bass.

Warren, J., Gelb, A., Horowitz, J., & Riordan, J. (2009). *One in 100: Behind bars in America 2008.* Washington, DC: Pew Charitable Trusts.

Western Interstate Commission for Higher Education. (2002). Tuition and fees in public higher education in the West, 2003-04, Table 6. IPEDS *College Opportunities On-Line (COOL)*. Retrieved November 22, 2010 from http://www .nces.ed.gov/ipeds/cool

Chapter V: Black Males, Media and Myths

There is no such thing in America as race transcendence.

Tavis Smiley, Huffington Post, 2008

May the best of your todays be the worst of your tomorrows.

Jay Z, "Young Forever," *The Blueprint 3,* 2009

The Art of Being Cool

Introduction

With the exception of a few notable Black men, including Kofi Anin, Eric Michael Dyson, Cornel West, and Tavis Smiley, most Americans' association with Black males has involved watching them achieve in sports or as criminals on the news. This has prompted popular culture to want to wear Black men's shoes, but fear to walk in the steps of one (Kelly, 1997). Although some aspects of American culture are Black (read "cool"), often the stereotypes that describe Black men are often the same things that define them. A large penis, physical prowess, and stylish apparel are cultural markers of Black men, along with quick to impregnate but slow to father, don't like to read, quick to get angry, and can't get a job. You can market Black males as cool, but you cannot market Black men in the job market.

Disparaging, depressing, and demoralizing perspectives are prevalent about Black males in America and their future. This has made popular culture's discussions of the race and character of Obama and new perceptions of the Black male among the most challenging and compelling conversations in both American and world history. The long-standing debate about race entered a new phase when the people of the United States elected Barack Obama president in 2008. This election in effect squashed questions of whether it is possible for a person of color to be elected president, but by no means did it end arguments over race and character. However, far from being a post-racial society as some have asserted, America has not resolved its largest obstacle to improving race relations: having a real, heartfelt discussion about the Black male.

This chapter seeks to redress this oversight through an examination of the role that myth has played in forming Black male identity. This chapter does not stand in the viewpoint that slavery was a myth; however, it serves as a rereading of the way myth has been woven into the tapestry of Black masculinity. This is a socio-historical, interpretive chapter, blending literary methods such as myth, cultural archetypes, and language to analyze social patterns used in the creation of perspectives on the identity of the Black man. While postcolonial in nature this chapter is not purely Afrocentric and has cross-cultural value, as African Americans are social trend indicators enacting behavioral patterns that lead Hispanic Americans by five to 10 years and lead European Americans by 10 to 15 years (Patterson, 1998).

Put simply, what happens in the African American community happens shortly thereafter in other ethnic communities in the United States. Additionally, since African Americans have been highly effective in endorsing social change in the United States and represent the first elected president in America who is Black and male, a study of Black masculinity is not only timely, it is necessary. In Dr. King's (1963) letter from the Birmingham jail he tells us, "We are [all] caught in an inescapable network of mutuality, tied in a single garment of destiny. Whatever affects one directly, affects all indirectly" (p. 1). In short, Black history *is* American history.

Theoretical Approach

There are many suitable theories to study on how historical and cultural myths apply socially and politically to Blacks in history. Postcolonial theory wrestles with European cultural influences on colonized people (Desi & Nair, 2005), and critical race theory deals with the legally and socially structured concepts of race and power (Tate, 1997). Another is Négritude, an approach that deals with rejecting European dominant colonialist attitudes toward Black French citizens (Césaire, 1997). Afrocentricity by Asante (2003) is another. However, postcolonial theory is not African- or African American-ethnocentric. Critical race theory in turn is silent about the use of myth in social identity. Finally, Négritude is largely about French nationalism and not inclusive of those who are of additional mixtures of African heritage.

Instead, this chapter argues for a blended theoretical approach. This approach uses critical race theory to inquire of the historical influences of myths and legends in forming male identity, postcolonial theory to examine current ideas that are influenced by both unconscious and conscious residual memories, and an emerging approach called "prolepsis" (Smyth, 1920), where the future is dealt with as if it were occurring today. These three theories taken together I call Janus.

The term *Janus* is taken from the Greek and Roman deity of the same name who is the god of new beginnings and the gatekeeper of all doors (Baumgartner, 1984). Koestler (1967) gives a deeper understanding of Janus based on the Greek word *holon* that will have direct relevance to this chapter. Janus is often sculpted and drawn as a two-headed figure similar to many two-headed African masks (Thompson, 1983, pp. 262-266). The two heads allow Janus to look not only at where he stands in relationship to his community of gods; it also allows him to look in the opposite direction, toward people. The Janus effect simultaneously sees the past and present to give views on the present. These insights can in turn be used to anticipate how the coming times will challenge, reinterpret, and restore the myth of the Black male and Black masculinity. In short, we can use the past—understood from a standpoint of a postcolonial theory and critical race theory—to examine current frameworks in conjunction with prolepsis, and to examine future interpretations of Black manhood and an African American president. In this example, President Obama can be viewed as the proleptical future of Black masculinity.

The Art of Being Cool

Historical Literature Review

In essence, a myth is an inherited relationship between social goals that may include change or preservation and current power relations (Halualani, 1997). Both religiously and socially framed, myths that are combined into a single story—a mythology—can define and inspire a people. A mythology usually contains an origin or creation of the world and society; it has a journey and a hero. A journey involves movement and movement implies progress (Solomon, 1979). A hero embodies all the idealized virtues of a society into one person in the form of a story that has dramatic elements, including a theme involving a fall and rise against the odds, such as the ones found in mythological stories about Adam, Moses, and Gilgamesh (Campbell, 1972). A hero is also a man who "stands up manfully against his father and in the end victoriously overcomes him" (Freud, 1939, p. 9). Stories and myths of heroes that are passed from one generation to the next result in what Sigmund Freud (1939) calls a *collective unconscious* (p. 170). Freud (1939) amplified this term as *phylogenetic inheritance,* "the mental residue of those primeval times has become a heritage which, with each new generation, needs only to be awakened, not reacquired" (p. 171). Carl Jung (1964) later called inherited unconscious symbols, thoughts, and images from the past that have meaning in the present a *cultural archetype.*

Despite the religious and social differences of the many cultures that exist all over the world, they all have common archetypes of birth and rebirth, flood, and rebellion against a father figure. Rebellion against the father is a ritual in totemism, the first form of religion we know of that includes laws and prohibition of sacrifice (Freud, 1939). Totemism alludes to symbolic rituals of a son taking the place of his father through sacrifice. Often in rituals, the father's blood is spilled, or the flesh is burned and consumed in the form of inhaling smoke from the fire. In a desire to take the place of the father, the realistic act of murdering the father became a symbolic ritual of a sacred animal sacrificed only at certain times (Freud). These forms of cannibalism were ritualistic, and did not always involve eating flesh (Patterson, 1998). The totems sometimes came in the form of a father's bones worn around the neck or the symbol of the father's spirit animal engraved on a piece of stone or wood.

A substitute for human sacrifice handed down from Abraham was the ritual of circumcision (Patterson) in which the foreskin of the male penis is cut off. "For the generations to come every male among you who is eight days old must be circumcised" (Genesis 17:12a, NIV). This is still practiced by followers of Abraham. Arabs circumcise at the age of 13 as a rite of passage into adulthood. By exposing the male organ, the rite of circumcision makes a symbolic link between masculinity and reproduction

72

Chapter V: Black Males, Media and Myths

(*Erasmus,* 1998). Circumcision is performed on women as well, usually as a means of restricting a woman's sexual activity since a woman's worth is tied to the control of reproduction and the management of property value (*Erasmus*). However, the majority of circumcisions are performed on men.

Male totems became articles of faith to be used only in specific ways. Breaking the rules for these rituals became taboo. To protect himself against a son and his ritual, a father castrated his son, killed his son, or expelled his son into the wilderness. Being thrust out of paradise into the wilderness is also referred to as the "lost garden" in feminist theology (Grey, 1999), from which masculinity studies branched. This paradise lost theme is often the start of a hero's journey and brings us to another common mythological cultural archetype: Genesis. Genesis is a fictional beginning that serves to incorporate a culture's values of the past into the present or a "yearning for a simpler, more harmonious style of life, an existence 'closer to nature'" (Marx, 1964, p. 6).

Historical Implications

If constant hypervigilance (Head, 2005) against physical abuse such as lynching and mental anguish from the haunting vestiges of slavery are not enough burdens to bear, African American men are the loneliest and unpartnered racial group in the world. Regardless of age, income level, and social success, African American men hold the lowest marriage rate among males in the United States (Patterson, 1998). This is not so for Black men in other parts in the world, who not only marry but stay involved with fatherhood. For African American men, neither marriage nor fatherhood is valued as a practice. Unwillingness to get married and lack of interest in parenting a child leave many women and children forsaken within the African American community. This may be the reason that over 70% of African American households are run with Black women as the head of the household (Morgan, 1999). This leaves African American boys and girls without an adult male role model to create traditional families and fosters reasons for rejection of biological fathers.

Unseen, unfamiliar, and unrehearsed patterns of productive spousal relationships result in distrust and even hatred between African American men and women (Cazenave & Smith, 1990). "This is so because the great majority of Afro-American mothers have been seduced, deceived, betrayed, and abandoned by the men to whom they gave their love and trust" (Patterson, 1998, p. 4). The men who sire their children often abandon African American women. This in turn leaves many women desperate to find men to support their children. Thirty percent of DNA paternity tests where the biological mother named the man as the biological father were proven false (Smith, 2008). For the small amount of American

73

men who do decide to marry, women in the United States are awarded sole custody 86% of the time in divorce custody cases (Bertoia & Drakich, 1993).

Whatever the reason for divorce, spousal abuse, neglect, or just unhappiness, the wife can remove the kids from the home and the husband is usually expected to pay child support (Horay, 1978). This means that even if the wife is unfaithful to her husband and petitions for divorce, the husband still has the obligation to pay child support often with no say-so in how the money is spent and without guarantee of visitation rights (Horay). It is not uncommon in the United States for a father to be the victim of divorce through no fault of his own and become bankrupt without even seeing his children after the wife and children leave. Child support can be up to 50% if not more of a person's net income (Smith, 2008). If a mother falsely identifies a man as being the father of a child, and the man is later determined not to be the biological father, she can still sue for continuous child support if she can show that he has an established pattern of payment. The courts' thinking in this matter stems from what is the best interest of the child. After custody battles, children often become withdrawn toward their absent parent regardless of the reason. Known as PAS (Parent Alienation Syndrome), this physiological condition is caused when children are subjected to exaggerated negative depictions of an absent parent, usually their father (Plumb & Lindley, 1990).

Fatherhood rights in America are extremely unfair toward men, even before the child is born. Men in the United States have little say in decisions of abortion (Bertoia & Drakich, 1993). Reproductive rights are strictly in the hands of women and men have little involvement except monetarily. It is no wonder that many men, especially African American men decide not to marry. However, this decision does not tend to lead African American women to abort pregnancies of absentee fathers. These are all reasons and consequences for perceptions of Black men as irresponsible fathers.

African American women frequently sacrifice their futures and young bodies out of loneliness, a desire for someone to love them, and the belief that their child will change the endless cycle of misogyny toward Black women. Unfortunately, this results in an abundance of households headed by single, female African Americans, many of whom harbor negative attitudes toward the young boys in the home while fostering bonding with the young daughters (Patterson, 1998). African American women stigmatize their boys while simultaneously spreading mistrust to their daughters by encouraging them to be distrustful toward men. For example, 51% of African American men go to church at least once a month (Patterson). This may suggest to potential life mates that

Chapter V: Black Males, Media and Myths

African American men attending church are stable, responsible, and hardworking. However, many Black women who have independent gender attitudes reject biblical views of women and see a male's regular attendance of church as a negative practice (Patterson). Clearly, what is desired is not always desirable. The statistically high lack of employment, the high accusable and conviction rate of Black men in the United States, and an imprisonment rate that is seven times higher than White males between the ages of 20 and 39 (Dyson, 2007) has not only been blamed for the poor life partner choices, but has become the standard for which many African American women settle. Additionally, African American women often have a fear of their black sons; they fear for the safety of their Black men and unconsciously "make babies of" their young sons and adult partners in an effort to protect them (Wesling, 1991, p. 92). This results in a continual cycle of unrealized emotional, independent development for many Black men and leads to socially reinforced irresponsibility.

Because many African American women feel there is a lack of available African American men, they are often forced to assume the lead role in the household and often unknowingly pass along economic marginalization and increased mental problems such as depression to their sons (Williams, et al., 2007). Environment alone is not responsible for mental health. Forty percent of African American men are known to be slow metabolizers of antidepressants (Satel, 2002), requiring doctors to adjust dosages differently for their Black patients than for their White patients.

Even when the children of unemployed and incarcerated Black men do not go to prison, they often start out economically disadvantaged (Dyson, 2007), and are emotionally challenged from having emotionally unavailable and physically absent fathers. This leads to a cyclical pattern of depression and feelings of hopelessness that often show up in the form of aggression (Head, 2005). This anger is then expressed violently by young boys in the home and toward other African Americans. The images of violence that classify Black men may be due in part to their physiological and sociological frustration. For many African Americans, an honorable death from protecting territory is an expected, common event all too often.

Gang involvement may not only provide communal family networks that take the place of absentee fathers, but may offer opportunities to prove manhood in otherwise impossible ways. Forced or voluntary suicides are common within the African American community throughout all age levels (Seiden, 1970). Similar to an urban jihad, African American men sacrifice their lives as symbols of rebellion against oppression by intentionally provoking extreme violent behavior in the hopes of being released from physiological bondage to the freedom of an honorable, quick death. These African American men sacrifice their lives for gang colors and territorial property rights. Not only does the practice of forced suicide become honorable, but when a Black male kills another Black male it often represents sacrificially killing himself (Wiegman, 1993). Many African American men sacrifice others when they cannot symbolically sacrifice their fathers whose identity is often unknown. Coincidentally, rejecting the father (when he is known and can be identified) has been shown to have a statistically high relationship to not only economic success but academic achievement as well (Patterson, 1998).

This section has examined African American male sacrifice of others and the sacrifice of the father. However, sacrifice of self often results in a sacrifice of health care and well-being for Blacks in America.

Sacrifice

For African American men who feel hopeless about the future, health care is just simply not important. One reason stems from the fact that many Black men in America resign themselves to a bleak future of marginalization and disenfranchisement. Another reason ascribed to the lack of attention to health care is the likelihood that African Americans males will be underemployed and over-incarcerated, leaving them unable to find jobs or jobs with health care benefits (Bonczar, 2003). For African Americans who are employed they often feel that hypertension is unavoidable for a Black man and just accept it as God's will, fatalistically believing that medications and treatments are futile (Rose, et al., 2000). In addition, Black men often are reluctant to miss work for preventive medical appointments once they do find a job (Kaplan & Rose, 1999). More related to "stable" Black men (at least on the surface) with traditional jobs, postcolonial-modeled ideas of Black masculinity advance the notion that a Black man is supposed to be physically able to handle anything. It is a social taboo for a Black man to show weakness in any form. Black men feel that they are "strong" and thus not at risk for illness; therefore, many see no need for regular checkups that could increase their life span (Blocker, et al., 2006).

Research also suggests that Black men frequently place the needs of their families ahead of themselves and often forgo their own health-related needs and appointments (Rose, et al., 2000). Black men do not see their views of the body, as sacred and connected to religious beliefs, reflected in American health care. African American men report they often feel their bodies are being invaded and on display in examining rooms, which results in fear

Chapter V: Black Males, Media and Myths

of going to the doctors because of anticipated racism (Blocker, et al., 2006). These opinions are not only based on distant racial memories passed down from one generation to the next, but by recent facts and experiences.

Older generations of African American men are keenly aware of the Study of Untreated Syphilis in the Male Negro, better known as the Tuskegee Experiment, and elders' memories and opinions about this have led to younger generations of African American men being more likely to believe that Blacks are the targets of medical and scientific experiments. In 1933, hundreds of Black men in Tuskegee, Alabama were intentionally and without their permission infected with syphilis and then denied treatment in an experiment to test progression of the disease (Brandt, 1978). This supports the reasoning behind the current generation of African Americans being more likely to believe that AIDS was created to destroy Blacks (Blocker, et al., 2006). This leads to a rejection of ethnic designer drugs such as the FDA-approved BiDil in 2005. Created as a race-specific treatment for heart failure among African American men, BiDil set the stage for medical ethics and ethnic debates (Kahn, 2004).

In addition to the ethical considerations of race-prescribed drugs, African American men are fearful of taking medication, even when the drugs are proven to be necessary. Black soldiers were shown to have a high incidence of hemolytic anemia when given malaria prophylaxis during World War II (Kalow, Goedde, & Agarwal, 1986). Sickle cell anemia is common among people from Africa, India, the Caribbean, the Middle East, and the Mediterranean because they all share a resistance to malaria (University of Utah, 2008). Those who had the lowest susceptibility to disease were more likely to survive on the slave ships from Africa. This means the very reason that their ancestors survived the Middle Passage is the same reason they are more susceptible to sickle cell anemia today. The very people who need it may never accept a drug crafted for those of Mediterranean descent. With an objectively reasonable distrust of health care practices toward Black men, information about AIDS has been known to be disseminated in private conversations among African Americans, outside earshot of European Americans.

The fact that Black men who are employed are likely to know another Black man that is unemployed, employed intermittently, incarcerated, or is unwed with children, has created the space for critical thinking of what it means to be a Black man. Many of the spaces where these conversations occur are in barbershops that Black men and boys frequent. Black barbershops are one of the few places where Black men of all ethnicities, age groups, employment statuses, occupations, and sexual orientations meet and have honest discussions that are not only possible but

The Art of Being Cool

encouraged. In a typical Black barbershop, conversations about Black masculinity center on survival within the Black community. Toughness, decisiveness, aggressiveness, violence, and powerful athletic prowess are all valued traits to Black men (Franklin, 1985). These tough-guy characteristics are sources of cultural capital that maintain acceptable ways to deal with racism and economic oppression (Oliver, 1989). Black men, many of whom have had no father in the home, have constructed their own definition of Black masculinity based on what they expect from themselves to survive (Franklin, 1985). Survival in this case means being able to navigate one's identity in terms related to economic opportunity. Both in the streets and in the boardroom, a readiness to fight is valued. More than intellect, physical prowess is the traditionally regarded aspect of Black manhood.

As we have discussed, many Black males choose to draw on their cultural wealth of physical pride and strength for the monetary and social capital that being an athlete entails. In other words, Black men sacrifice their intelligence in favor of the hypermasculine, or "supermasculine menial" (Cleaver, 1968, p. 162) reinforced image of the Black athlete. By far, the African American basketball player is the most culturally accepted athlete. The basketball player does not wear a football helmet; thus you can see his face, and he doesn't wear the long sleeves and pants of baseball players, so his uniform does not cover up his body. This makes the basketball player more visible in advertisements (Boyd & Shropshire, 2000). Originally sold on the auction block, now Black bodies are on display; they're product-endorsing commodities, easily available for public consumption (Alexander, 1994). In basketball and in other sports Black men often risk their health for the pursuit of financial gain. Not only is this accepted, athletic prowess is expected of Black men in America. Highly profitable sports and other types of risk-taking behavior concerning the body are reflected in other areas of Black masculinity, such as unprotected sex.

Unprotected sex, which frequently leads to HIV/AIDS and other sexually transmitted diseases, is one of the leading causes of death within the Black community (Lemelle, Harrington, & LeBlanc, 2000). Whether from women who contracted AIDS from other men who have HIV/AIDS or from instances when men succumb to pressure and find solace, acceptance, and understanding from intimate relations with other men, unprotected sex is risky behavior. Black men who are publicly heterosexual while privately having sex with men are blamed for much of the spread of HIV/AIDS. Also known as the "down low" (King, 2004), these men then carry the AIDS virus to their wives and girlfriends. While these claims have been refuted somewhat (Ford, Hall, Kaufman, & Thrasher, 2007), this type of sexual behavior remains a reason for high rates of sexually transmitted disease among Black women;

Chapter V: Black Males, Media and Myths

in addition, the "down low" has damaged the self-esteem of many gay Black men. Negative attitudes toward gay men are advanced by writings in the book of Leviticus: "Do not have sexual relations with a man as one does with a woman; that is detestable" (18:22, NIV). As a result, Black men who are gay are forced to secretly deny their true feelings and carry out cultural "expectations *for* men while secretly submitting to their personal attractions *to* men" (emphasis in the original; Pitt, 2006, p. 257). Black men who are gay face not only negative racial conceptions of being Black, but also must confront internal, immoral conflicts about being gay as well.

The Future of Black Manhood

In large part due to Obama, current conceptions of Black masculinity call for remembering the past while simultaneously creating spaces for individuality and cultural diversity for the future. Surviving slavery and fighting oppression are not to be forgotten, but to be used as learning tools for the future (Du Bois, 1915, p. xx). In this regard, if we view Obama as the genesis of what is not a new but finally recognized model of Black manhood, then we subscribe to the notion that traditional ideas of Black masculinity are going to be remade, reinterpreted, and reshaped in new ways. Black men will no longer have to choose between being unpartnered and unwed. Black men will no longer have to choose between depression and despair. Black men will no longer have to choose between being popular and smart. Either alone, side by side with his wife Michelle, or in a picture with his two daughters, Obama's depiction in the American media will surely be a new hallmark for Black men. For example, Obama is not only an intellectual; he carries his physicality with confidence. He body surfs and looks good doing it. He smiles. He makes it evident that he loves his wife, our First Lady. The First Family represents a traditional, intact nuclear family, with the addition of a man playing an active, emotionally available part, not a breadwinner-only role or a submissive, mostly absent role. These are just a few of the counter-interpretive depictions of not only Black men but Black families typically depicted in mainstream media.

As we see from the influence of hip-hop and sports in the media, being American means being inclusive of Black culture. Transcending both space and time (Brown, 2008), Black identity does not have to change with each circumstance and place. When we see Obama on national television we cannot help noticing that he is as Black when he is in a Chicago neighborhood as he is with heads of state. African American culture and language are now part of mainstream society, allowing the current generation to experiment and play with Black identity in ways their parents never dreamed of, often at the expense of White Americans (Neal, 2002). Obama successfully navigates culture in a way that creates space for people of different cultures to feel comfortable. Navigating one's culture in society is at the heart of Black masculinity (Boyd, 1997). Because of Obama, Black masculinity does not have to hide behind an invisible, stoic mask.

Drawing on the rich cultural experience of being Black in America is where African American men draw their strength. Through emotional support and resourcefulness, Black men in America have developed adaptive traditions and practices (Lamm, 2003). It is this African American cultural practice of recognizing differences in others and not ignoring them which Black men use for empowerment. Du Bois (1903) called this ability *"two-ness"* or *double consciousness*. The idea is rooted in the belief that African Americans may be able to look at their experiences with a "divided self" and to see the world through multiracial eyes—an intuitiveness that enables them to perceive society from a unique moral perspective. This double consciousness, an outcome of slavery, empowered those who struggled with the institution's residual impact. Similar to Janus, *double consciousness* allows African Americans the ability to look past their horrible origins as slaves in America toward the future of what America should be. From a prolepsis perspective, African American men can rise from the dust of historically overlooked potential and break the bonds of slavery to stand among America's great leaders. Obama's election to the presidency and his successful election to a second term continues the role Black men in America have played by fulfilling the reinterpretation of the Declaration of Independence to include all of America's people.

For certain, President Obama's second term will have to deal with the deficit, foreign investors, immigration, and many other challenges. But the future will define today as a time of influences. Prior to President Obama's first election he stated, "I have not missed a parent-teacher conference since I've been president, and I didn't miss a parent-teacher conference when I was a candidate for president. And Michelle goes to all of those activities. We stay in constant contact with their [daughters Malia and Sasha] teachers" (Baker, 2010, p. 124). New co-parenting models such as the ones the First Family have provided can influence Americans in many ways. Previous to President Obama, most media portrayals of African American men in movies and television tended to show them likely to be involved in criminal activity (Miller & Maiter, 2008). Black fathers have been historically described as ineffective (Frazer & Frazer, 1993), and as contributors to a negative pathology of poor parenting (Moynihan, 1965). Additionally, Dates and Stroman (2001) assert that minoritized families are typically not portrayed accurately by media. Just the depictions of President Obama as a Black male who is not only a world leader but an actively involved father as well will have positive implications for African American families.

Chapter V: Black Males, Media and Myths

The myth of the Black male as a bad father will wane in prominence.

In addition, in the future we will look at President Obama's first and second terms in office as the moment in history when Black men got their act together. Or put in another way, the world will realize that Black men have had their act together for a long time. President Obama's time in office will inspire the varied, many Black men in America to work and think collectively. Those African Americans who made their fortunes as athletes will invest in education and industries that will benefit all of America. They will have taken the lead from business magnate George Soros and New York City Mayor Michael Bloomberg and will invest in Black males (Shah & Sato, 2012). In general, Americans will have realized that investing in Black males is just one way to reduce the national deficit and to shore up money in the depleting Social Security system. Also, in the future people will look at 2012 as the year that prompted people of color not only to run for political office, but to get elected. America will wake up to the fact that people of color are more than billboards or postcards; they are people with integrity.

When I hear people say that Obama was the best presidential candidate because of the content of his character and not because of the color of his skin, it pains me. I agree with the sentiment, but I disagree with the implication. To say that character alone was the overwhelming reason is akin to saying that for 200 years and 43 presidents, no one else of color had character worthy of the presidency. It is similar to saying we should ignore the hard work and sweat of the many minorities that helped build this country. In an article written before Obama's historic presidential victory, a columnist wrote:

> But we are a people as practical as we are dreamy. We'll soon remember that the country is in a deep ditch, and that we turned to the black guy not only because we hoped he would lift us up but because he looked like the strongest leader to dig us out. (Rich, 2008)

I take this to mean that it is precisely Obama's race that made him the best candidate in the presidential election. African Americans and minorities in America have experience with postcolonial issues and economic hardships. The character of Black masculinity in particular has a reputation of being strong. For is not character a vessel in which one places heritage, history, and heart?

To use the hybrid concept of Janus in another way, remember that Janus is also a gatekeeper. He opens doors. The appeal of the Janus effect is that it is a continuous cycle. It allows for critical thinkers to examine the past and present in terms of how the future affects today. Janus is a symbol of conscious change, as well as the god of new beginning. On January 20, 2012, the first month of the New Year, Obama was sworn in for the second time as president of the United States. He used the same Bible that Abraham Lincoln used when he was sworn in. This action completed a cycle of new beginnings, as Lincoln set the stage for African Americans to be elected into political office. Additionally, Lincoln was born 200 years before this important moment, in 1809. Is it any wonder that the month of January is named after the god Janus?

References

Afrika, L. (1993). *African holistic health.* Brooklyn: A&B Books.

Alexander, E. (1994). *"Can you be black and look at this?" Reading the Rodney King video(s).* New York: Whitney Museum of American Art.

Apel, D. (2004). *Imagery of lynching: Black men, white women, and the mob.* New Brunswick, NJ: Rutgers University Press.

Arias, D. C. (2007). High rate of incarcerated Black men devastating to family health. *The Nation's Health Article.* Hyattsville, MD: Center for Health Statistics.

Arias, E., & Smith, B. (2003). Deaths: Preliminary data for 2001. Hyattsville, MD: National Center for Health Statistics.

Asante, M. K. (2003). *Afrocentricity: The theory of social change.* Chicago: African American Images.

Ashcroft, B., Griffiths, G., and Tiffin, H. (1995). *The post-colonial studies reader.* London: Routledge.

Baker, B. (March, 2010). America's teachable moment. *Essence, 40*(11).

Baumgartner, A. (1984). *A comprehensive dictionary of the gods: From Abaast to Zvoruna.* New York: Wing Books.

Bertoia, C., & Drakich, J. (December, 1993). The father's rights movement. *Journal of Family Issues, 14*(4), 592-615.

Blocker, D., Romocki, L., Thomas, K., Jones, B., Jackson, E., Reid, L, & Campbell, M. (August, 2006). Knowledge, beliefs and barriers associated with prostate cancer prevention and screening behaviors among African-American men. *Journal of the National Medical Association 98*(8), 1286–1295.

Bonczar, T. P. (2003). *Prevalence of imprisonment in the U.S. population, 1974-2001.* Washington, DC: U.S. Department of Justice.

The Art of Being Cool

Boyd, T. (1997). *Am I black enough for you: Popular culture from the 'hood and beyond.* Bloomington, IN: Indiana University Press. Boyd, T., & Shropshire, K.L. (2000). *Basketball Jones: America above the rim.* New York: New York University Press.

Braden, W. (1975). Myths in a rhetorical context. *Southern Speech Communication Journal, 40*(2), 113-126.

Brandt, A. M. (1978). Racism and research: The case of the Tuskegee Syphilis Study. *Hastings Center Report, 8*(6), 21-29.

Browder, A. (1996). *Survival strategies for Africans in America.* Washington, DC: The Institute of Karmic Guidance.

Brown, M. C. (2000). Prophets of power in the professoriate: A sermon for cultural workers. In M. C. Brown & J. Davis (Eds.), *Black sons to mothers: Compliments, critiques, and challenges for cultural workers.* New York: Peter Lang Publishers.

Brown, T. J. (2008). "I am who I am": Black masculinity and the interpretation of individualism in the film *Barbershop. Qualitative Research Reports in Communication, 9*(1), 46-61.

Brundage, W. (1993). *Lynching in the new South: Georgia and Virginia 1880-1930.* Urbana: University of Illinois Press.

Budge, E. A. W. (1932). *The Queen of Sheba and her only son Menyelek (I).* London: Oxford University Press.

Bukhari, S. *Hadith.* Volume 6, Book 60, Number 435: USC. Retrieved December 16, 2008 from http://www.usc .edu/schools/college/crcc/engagement/resources/texts/muslim/hadith/bukhari/060.sbt.html

Burke, K. (1969). *A grammar of motives.* Berkeley: University of California Press.

Campbell, J. (1972). *The hero with a thousand faces.* Princeton, NJ: Princeton University Press.

Cazenave, N. & Smith, R. (1990). Gender differences in the perception of Black male-female relationships and stereotypes. In H. E. Cheatham and J. B. Stewart (Eds.), *Black families: Interdisciplinary perspectives.* New Brunswick, NJ: Transaction Books.

Chapter V: Black Males, Media and Myths

Césaire, A. (1997). *Return to my native land*. Newcastle Upon Tyne, UK: Bloodaxe Books.

Chapman, R., & Rutherford, J. (Eds.). (1988). *Male order: Unwrapping Masculinity*. London: Lawrence and Wishart.

Cleaver, E. (1968). *Soul on ice*. New York: Delta Books.

Cross, W. E., & Strauss, L. (1998). The everyday functions of African American identity. In J. K. Swim & C. Stangor (Eds.), *Prejudice: The target's perspective* (pp. 267-279). San Diego: Academic Press.

Dates, J. L., & Stroman, C. (2001). Portrayals of families of color on television. In J. Bryant & J. A. Bryant (Eds.), *Television and the American family*. Mahwah, NJ: Erlbaum.

Derdeyn, A. P. (Fall, 1978). Child custody: A reflection of cultural change. *Journal of Clinical Child Psychology*, 7(3), 169-173. doi: 10.1080/15374417809532833

Desi, G., & Nair, S. (2005). *Postcolonialisms: An anthology of cultural theory and criticism*. Oxford, UK: Berg Publishers.

Douglass, F. (2006). *What, to the slave, is the fourth of July?* New York: Dover Publications.

Du Bois, W. E. B. (1903). *The soul of Black folks*. New York: Dover Publications.

Du Bois, W. E. B. (1915). *The Negro*. New York: Holt.

Dyson, M. (2007). *Debating race with Michael Eric Dyson*. New York: Basic Civitas Books.

Engen, T. (1991). *Odor, sensation and memory*. New York: Praeger.

Erasmus, P. A. (1998). *Perspectives on Black masculinity: The abortion debate in South Africa. South African Journal of Ethnology, 21*, 203–206.

Every, G. (1970). *Christian mythology*. London: Hamlyn Publishing Group.

Ford, C. L., Whetten, K. D., Hall, S.A., Kaufman, J. S., & Thrasher, A. D. (2007). Black sexuality, social construction, and research targeting "the down low." *Annals of Epidemiology, 17*(3), 209-216.

Foundation, F. C. (2007). What we do [electronic version]. *If the World Were a Village of 100 People*. Retrieved December 16, 2008 at http://www.familycare.org/news/if_the_world .htm

Franklin, C. W. (1985). The Black male urban barbershop as a sex-role socialization setting. *Sex Roles, 12*, 965-979.

Frazer, J., & Frazer, T. (1993). *Father knows best* and *The Cosby show:* Nostalgia and the sitcom tradition. *Journal of Popular Culture, 27*(3), 163-172.

Fredrickson, G. M. (1987). *The black image in the white mind: The debate on Afro-American character and destiny 1817-1914*. Middletown, CT: Wesleyan University Press.

Freud, S. (1939). Moses and monotheism. London: Hogarth Press.

Ginsburg, R. (1962). *100 years of lynching*. New York: Lancer Books.

Goldenberg, D. (2003). *The curse of Ham: Race and slavery in early Judaism, Christianity, and Islam*. Princeton, NJ: Princeton University Press.

Goode, E. (1984). *Deviant behavior*. Englewood Cliffs, NJ: Prentice Hall.

Grey, M. (1999). "Expelled again from Eden": facing difference through connection. *Feminist Theology, 7*, 8-20.

Hall, J. D. (1993). *Revolt against chivalry: Jesse Daniel Ames and the women's campaign against lynching*. New York: Columbia University Press.

Halualani, R. (1997). *A sovereign nation's functional mythic discourse*. Thousand Oaks, CA: Sage Publications.

Head, J. (2005). *Black men and depression: Saving our lives, healing our families and friends*. New York: Harlem Moon Broadway Books.

Hine, D. C. (1994). *Hine sight: Black women & the reconstruction of American history*. Brooklyn: Carlson Publishing.

Horay. D. A. (Fall, 1978). Child custody: A reflection of cultural change. *Journal of Clinical Child Psychology, 7*(3), 169.

Howard, W. L. (1903). The Negro as a distinct ethnic factor in civilization. *Medicine 10*, 420-433.

Jameson, F. (1981). *The political unconscious: Narratives as a socially symbolic act.* Ithaca, NY: Cornell University Press.

Jay Z. (2009). Young forever. *The Blueprint 3.* Beverly Hills, CA: Roc Nation and Sony Music Entertainment.

Jefferson, T. (1776). Declaration of Independence: The unanimous declaration of the thirteen United States of America. *The Constitution Society.* Retrieved December 16, 2008 from http://www.constitution.org/usdeclar.htm

Jung, C. G. (1964). *Man and his symbols.* New York: Anchor Books, Doubleday.

Kahn, J. (2004). How a drug becomes ethnic. *Yale Journal of Health Policy, Law, and Ethics, 4*(1), 1-46.

Kalow, W., Goedde, H., & Agarwal, D. (1986). Aldehyde oxidation: ethnic variations in metabolism and response. In W. Kalow, H. Goedde, & D. Agarwal (Eds.), *Ethnic differences in reactions to drugs and xenobiotics* (pp. 113-138). New York: Alan R. Liss.

Kaplan, V., & Rose, B. (1999). Treatment of hypertension in blacks. Wolters Kluwer: Up to date. Retrieved January 31 from http://www.uptodate.com/contents/treatment-of-hypertension-in-blacks?source=search_result&search=Thiazide+diuretics&selectedTitle=20~150

Katznelson, I. (2005). *When affirmative action was white: An untold history of racial inequality in twentieth-century America.* New York: W. W. Norton.

Kelly, R. (1997). *Yo' mama's disfunktional! Fighting the culture wars in urban America.* Boston: Beacon Press.

King, J. L. (2004). *On the down low.* New York: Broadway.

King, M. L. (1963). *Letter from a Birmingham jail.* Madison, WI: University of American History.

Koestler, A. (1967). *The ghost in the machine.* London: Arkana.

Kunjufu, J. (1988). *To be popular or smart: The Black peer group.* Chicago: African American Images.

Lake, R. A. (1984). Order and disorder in anti-abortion rhetoric: A logological view. *Quarterly Journal of Speech, 70,* 425-443.

Lamm, K. (2003). Visuality and Black masculinity in Ralph Ellison's *Invisible Man* and Romare Bearden's photo-montages. *Callaloo, 26*(3), 813–835.

Lemelle, A., Harrington C., & LeBlanc, A. (Eds.). (2000). *Readings in the sociology of AIDS.* Upper Saddle River, NJ: Prentice Hall.

Lincoln, N. (1994). *Handbook of qualitative research.* Thousand Oaks, CA: Sage Publications.

Littlefield, K. Race. Huffington Post. http://www.huffington post .com/2008/07/21/tavis-smiley-tackles-obam_n_ 114160.html

Lydston, F. C. (1906). Castration instead of lynching. *Atlanta Journal-Record of Medicine, 8,* 457.

Marshall, F. (1967). *Labor in the South.* Cambridge, MA: Harvard University Press.

Marx, L. (1964). *The machine in the garden: Technology and the pastoral ideal in America.* Oxford, UK: Oxford University Press.

Mauss, M. (1990). *The gift: forms and functions of exchange in archaic societies.* London:Routledge.

McBride, D. (1973). Final report of the Tuskegee Syphilis Study ad hoc advisory panel. Milestone Documents. Accessed January 31, 2013 from http://www.milestone documents .com/documents/view/final-report-of-the-tuskegee- syphilis-study-ad-hoc-advisory-panel

Meeropol, A. (1939). *Strange fruit.* Commodore Records.

Miller, W., & Maiter, S. (2008). Fatherhood and culture: Moving beyond stereotypical understandings. *Journal of Ethnic & Cultural Diversity in Social Work, 17*(3), 279-300.

Mizell, A. (1999). Life course influences on African men's depression adolescent parental composition, self-concept, and adult earning. *Journal of Black Studies, 29*(4).

Morgan, J. (1999). *When chicken-heads come home to roost: A hip-hop feminist breaks it down.* New York: Touchstone.

Moynihan, D. P. (1965). Employment, income and the ordeal of the Negro family. *Daedalus, 94,* 745-770.

Neal, M. A. (2002). *Soul babies: Black popular culture and the post-soul aesthetic.* New York: Routledge.

Oliver, W. (1989). Sexual conquest and patterns of Black-on-Black violence: A structural cultural perspective. *Violence and Victims, 4,* 257-273.

Page, C. (August 17, 2008). Obama vs. bigots and "swift books" [electronic version]. *Real Clear Politics.* Retrieved December 17, 2008 from http://www.realclearpolitics .com/articles/2008/08/obama_vs_bigots_and_ swift_ book.html

Patterson, O. (1998). *Rituals of blood: Consequences of slavery in two American centuries.* New York: Basic Civitas Books.

Pederson, J. P., & Smith J. C. (1995). *African American break-throughs: 500 years of Black firsts.* New York: UXL.

Pitt, R. N. (2006). Downlow mountain? De/stigmatizing bisexuality through pitying and pejorative discourses in media. *The Journal of Men's Studies, 14*(2), 254-258.

Plumb, G., & Lindley, M. (1990). *Humanizing child custody disputes: The family's team.* Springfield, IL: Charles C. Thomas Publishing.

Rakow, L. (1992). *Women making meaning: New feminist directions in communication.* New York: Routledge.

Rich, F. (November 1, 2008). Guess who's coming to dinner? *The New York Times.* http://www.nytimes.com/2008/11/02/ opinion/ 02rich.html?pagewanted=all&_r=0

Rose, L., Kim, M., Dennison, C., & Hill, M. (2000). The contexts of adherence for African Americans with high blood pressure. *Journal of Advanced Nursing, 32*(3), 595.

Satel, S. (May 5, 2002). I am a racially profiling doctor. *The New York Times Magazine.* http://www.nytimes.com/2002/ 0505/magazine/05PROFILE.html

Seiden, R. (1970). We're driving young black men to suicide. *Psychology Today, 4,* 24-28.

Shah, S., & Sato, G. (October, 2012). *Where Do We Go from Here? Philanthropic Support for Black Men and Boys.* New York: Open Society Foundations. Available at http://www. foundationcenter.org/gainknowledge/research/pdf/osf bmb.pdf

Smith, C. (2008). Carnell Smith, pfv. http://www.carnellsmith .com/Biography

Smyth, H. W. (1920). *Greek grammar.* Cambridge, MA: Harvard University Press.

Solomon, M. (1979). The positive woman's journey: A mythic analysis of the rhetoric of stop ERA. *The Quarterly Journal of Speech, 65,* 262-274.

Stroman, C. A. (November, 2005). Disseminating HIV/AIDS information to African Americans. *Journal of Health Care for the Poor and Underserved, 16*(4), Supplement B, 24-37.

Tate, W. F. (1997). Critical race theory and education: History, theory, and implications. *Review of Research in Education, 22,* 195-247.

Thompson, R. F. (1983). *Flash of the spirit.* New York: Random House.

University of Utah. (2008). What is sickle cell disease? Retrieved December 12, 2008 from http://learn .genetics.utah.edu/ content/disorders/whataregd/sicklecell

Weigmann, K. (March, 2006). Racial medicine: Here to stay? *EMBO Reports, 7*(3), 246-249.

Wesling, F. C. (1991). *The Isis papers: The keys to the colors.* Chicago: Third World Press.

Wiegman, R. (1993). *Feminism, "the boyz" and other matters regarding the male.* London: Routledge.

Williams, D. R., et al. (March, 2007). Prevalence and distribution of major depressive disorder in African Americans, Caribbean blacks, and non-Hispanic whites: Results from the National Survey of American Life. *Archives of General Psychiatry, 64*(3), 305-315.

Chapter VI: Hip-Hop and Masculinity

*See I don't bend and I won't rust and I don't break and I won't
bust.*

Rakim, "What's On Your Mind?"

House Party II Soundtrack, 1991

*Because the streets is a short stop/
Either you're slingin' crack rock or you got a wicked jump shot.*

Notorious B.I.G., "Things Done Changed,"

Ready to Die, 1994

*All I need is one mic, one beat, one stage,
one n*gga frontin' my face on the front page,
only if I had one gun, one girl and one crib,
one God to show me how to do things his son did.*

Nas & Chucky Thompson, "One Mic,"

Stillmatic, 2002

*Don't have to blow twenty thou' to get to know honey's style.
Show her the town;
steal her heart, no money down.*

Rakim, "When I B on the Mic,"

The Master, 1999

I'm not a player I just crush a lot.

Big Pun, "Still Not a Player,"

Capital Punishment, 1998

The Art of Being Cool

Introduction

Hip-hop is a global phenomenon. Hip-hop is cool. If researchers are to take a serious look at hip-hop then they must start paying attention to the common social themes that create and continue the international popularity of this music and its influence on masculinity—all types of masculinity, including males who are not Black. It cannot be denied that the face of modern masculinity is represented by the Black male and hip-hop is his soundtrack. However, hip-hop is about more than just thugs and jeans. Diddy, aka Sean Jean "Puffy" combs has a line of designer suits named after him and hip-hop mogul Jay Z has been known to wear a business suit now and again. Both men are well-known hip-hoppers and both run extremely successful, multifaceted businesses.

Katz and Earp (1999) assert that the phenomenon of hip-hop involves much more than the mere fact that White boys are imitating Black boys, and Black boys are not just copying Italian gangsters. What is really happening is that young boys and young men of all races are looking for representations of contemporary masculinity. Even Italian gangsters copied the first organized crime organization, Irish gangsters. If we look closely, young ethnic boys tend to gravitate toward what is thought of as tough, masculine and in control; that is, they like what is cool. It is not the color of the person they are imitating, it is his resilience and ability to be manly. The last 150 years have done away for the most part with job apprenticeships and rites of passage among groups of Black males. As the world becomes more Westernized, rituals that transmit cultural expectations that are crucial to ethnic identity and masculinity have been abandoned for many young men.

Using the theoretical approach of rites of passage, we focus on *separation,* where plebs are set apart from ordinary life and engage in rites of segregation or *acts of transition* also called *marge* or "limen," which incorporate the threshold or simultaneously occupied spaces between past, present, and future. Young men-to-be also engage in rites of initiation—*agreation*—in which youths are reintroduced to society as full members (van Gennep, 1960). This chapter asserts that hip-hop has taken the place of adolescent masculinity rituals for young boys all over the world, including young Black males.

Research on adolescence and music often blames hip-hop for almost everything wrong with today's youth. For example, it has been suggested that adolescents who have school-related

Chapter VI: Hip-Hop and Masculinity

behavioral problems have a preference for rap [hip-hop] music as well as high incidences of sexual activity, drug and alcohol abuse, and arrests (Epstein, Pratto, & Skipper, 1990). However, researchers also note that adolescent delinquency problems may just be a result of behaviors associated with being an adolescent (Took & Weiss, 1994), and that music "is a reflection of the social environment . . . and simply reflects already existing adolescent sentiments back to the youth subculture" (Epstein, et al., 1990, p. 382). It may be that problem behaviors, such as adolescent drug abuse and violence, can be seen as risk-taking conduct through which adolescents sometimes turn to test their potential and prove their individuality, and not a result of the music they listen to. In fact, adolescent delinquency has been a longtime concern for social science scholars, even before hip-hop began. It is an interest rooted in the knowledge that in the United States alone, an estimated 1,234 youths run away from home and 2,255 teenagers drop out of school every day (Edelman, 1995).

This suggests the transition from adolescence to adulthood in Western-influenced societies like the United States is difficult. Prior social science investigations that looked at adolescent delinquency and youth identity issues focused on the negative effects of hip-hop (Hansen, 1995). However, the view of hip-hop as a modern day rite of passage and positive rational tool may present a different picture. This chapter focuses on "adolescence" as traced from the Latin word *adolescens*, which means a starting point or initiation into the period or state of transformation of a child into an adult (Bendix, 1970). This definition indicates ambiguity in a person's life which is often marked by conflicting societal responsibilities that often cause confusion. For example, the U.S. Supreme Court has ruled that policy makers can impose both responsibilities and punishments on adolescence and at the same time ignore the fact that they are youths (Males, 1999). While the terms "youth," "young adult," "juvenile," and "teenager" refer to the age group between childhood and adult, "adolescence" by definition refers to a transitional process and not just to an age-related range of numbers. In the Western world, "we have a comparatively 'riteless' society for adolescents, with a distinct lack of guidance or healthy opportunities for forging one's identity" (Maddern, 1990). This is true despite the fact that we know societies with clearly identifiable and culturally legitimated rites of passage have lower incidents of adolescent delinquency (Bloch & Niederhoffer, 1958). The transitional path to adulthood needs to be taken seriously. Adolescence means change and is therefore suitable to study within the framework of rites of passage.

93

The Art of Being Cool

Literature Review

As I have shown, academic attention has been placed on adolescents and the need for peer social acceptance, adolescent gang participation, and the relationship between adolescence and music. This interest was born out of the realization that because of changing social structures, ideas of marriage and family have changed as well. Family social structures instill morals and values, and the way values are passed to children can be indicators of adolescent delinquency (Tarry & Emler, 2007). Because of the underutilization of rites of passage in the West, transitional periods between adolescence and adulthood give insights to how rites of passage dampen violent behavior (Blimankrantz & Gavazzi, 1993). Interest was also paid specifically to Black adolescence (McKenry, Everett, Ramseur, & Carter, 1989), since many minorities appear frustrated and confused as they wrestle with low self-esteem and bruised feelings about their ethnic identity (Alford, 2003).

Many minoritized adolescents feel so left out of contemporary society that the desire to belong to a social group becomes a driving motive to join gangs (Baumeister & Leary, 1995). These peer influences create emotional support for the fragmented social structures in which many adolescents live (Payne & Cornwell, 2007). Papachristos (1998) researched gang involvement and rites of passage. He found that gangs provide adolescents with a group of elders, a period of separation, a sacred place or territory, symbolic death trials, and ritual trials as well as reincorporation into the community. Gang involvement mirrors hip-hop in many ways, especially since many of its founders were indeed gang members. Gangs are *urban tribes*—micro-groups that share common interests or worldviews, dress, and behavioral patterns (Maffesoli, 1996). Similar to Hebdige's (1979) study of enclaves and punk rockers, research announces that modern urban subgroups are often a result of not having a father figure in the home, especially among many African American youth (King, Harris, & Heard, 2004; Hofferth, Pleck, Stueve, Bianchi, & Sayer, 2002; Lerman & Sorensen, 2000). The lack of a male figurehead at home reflects a lack of structure and lack of opportunity to pass on male-related familial values.

Adolescent music research does not tend to focus just on hip-hop. Studies have also examined rock and hip-hop and found that in both genres, adolescent listeners' behavior may just be actions that are associated with the fact that the listeners are adolescent males (Took & Weiss, 1994). This supports research indicators that suggest hip-hop and its influence of gang-related themes is merely a reflection of the times (Epstein, Pratto, & Skipper, 1990). Social gatherings for many adolescents usually involve alcohol as part of ritualistic behavior in locations as far from the United States as Norway (Sande, 2002). Drugs, including

Chapter VI: Hip-Hop and Masculinity

alcohol are part of experimentation for youth all over the world. Although this information is interesting and insightful, it points out a need for research on how hip-hop functions as a rite of passage to dissuade feelings of inferiority and misplacement for adolescents who need rituals to transition into adulthood for emotional and social recognition.

Methodology

A comprehensive search was conducted using the Academic Search Premier database and entering the terms "hip-hop", "global hip-hop", and "international hip-hop". These terms were then refined to facilitate searches by country and ethnicity for academic journal articles on: "African hip-hop", "Asian hip-hop", "Australian hip-hop", "French hip-hop", "German hip-hop", etc., to explore the degree to which this genre of music has become a global phenomenon among adolescent males. These terms were then looked at through the lens of cultural rites of passage for each country. It is important to note that most of the information on Latin hip-hop focuses on reggaetone, which by definition is not hip-hop and was discarded. However, Latin American hip-hop is addressed in the American hip-hop section.

Theoretical Framework

Although there are many theories related to hip-hop, this chapter focuses its research through the lens of limen, the middle segment of rites of passage that is synonymous with being in a transitional state. Media cultivation theory, which postulates that people's view of the world is often based on the media (Gerbner, Gross, Morgan, & Signorielli, 1986), is one such theory discussed here. Another is distinctiveness theory, which suggests that ethnic identity is more obvious for minoritized ethnic groups than members of an ethnic majority (Brewer, 1991; McGuire, McGuire, Child, & Fujioka, 1978). Because of globalization and music videos accessible online and via mobile devices, hip-hop has reached the homes of countless people around the world. This means that much of the broadcast symbols and values depicted in hip-hop videos encourage viewers to model and adopt the behavior depicted in the videos to which people are exposed. Hip-hop music videos have become a staple of modern popular culture, often superseding the music itself (Aufderheide, 1986). Because of technology and modern mass media, hip-hop has spread extensively throughout areas that habitually relied on oral traditions to carry messages (McLuhan, 1962). Researchers in turn focus on aspects of hip-hop that they feel are similar or important to them, such as ethnicity or race. However, media cultivation theory and the idea of a global village do little to explain the specific, culturally selected symbols or values in the media that adolescents—who are in an ambiguous social and self-defining position in society—particularly use. Nor does distinctiveness theory explicate the social and ethnic aspects that viewers adopt, how these aspects function, or how adolescents express their interpretations. Rites of passage may help find the connection between masculinity and media.

In society, rites of passage are comprised of three phases: *rites of separation,* where plebs are set apart from ordinary life; *rites of segregation or acts of transition*—also known as *marge* or limen—that incorporate the threshold or simultaneously occupied spaces between past, present, and future; and *rites of initiation*—agreation—where members are reintroduced to society as full members (van Gennep, 1960). For van Gennep, rites of passage encapsulate a broad range of ritual events such as handling sociological and physical boundaries that include age, and dealing with metaphorical boundaries that include traditional societal views (Winthrop, 1991). Van Gennep became fascinated with rites of passage while studying tribes in Africa. He noted that the same symbolic rites of passage found in Africa were similar to those in other parts of the world. These cultural archetypes (Jung, 1966) found around the world prove identities related to occupation that include ideology, and interpersonal relationships are decisive in adolescent ethnic identity (Steinberg, 1993; McKenry, Everett, Ramseur, & Carter, 1989). How the past relates to the future, life and death, and how new participants fit into society are common themes around the world regardless of ethnic or cultural ideology.

Rites of segregation, the second phase in rites of passage, were of particular interest to Turner (1979). He expanded this component which van Gennep called limen. Limen, or the adjective liminal, means the stage where one is betwixt-and-between two states, such as the space between childhood and adolescence (Turner, 1974). Turner further tells us that liminal states such as these transcend social status, creating alienation, distance, inequality, and exploitation for all who are in a state of change (1974). These liminal rituals often serve as motivation that temporarily transcends fixed social structures and breaks free of established limits.

While it may seem that adhering to rituals is an action that supports social expectations, in reality liminal rituals are "ritual anti-structure[s]" (Schwartz, 1972, p. 904), that preserve social structures by allowing initiates the space in which to experiment and play with ideas about identity. Ritual challenges the dominant power structure in ways not usually recognized (Alexander, 1991). Liminal rituals allow for a form of catharsis, draining off or deflecting hostility toward the status quo (Schwartz, 1972). Hip-hop works as a liminal rite of passage for adolescent youth to create their own identities by managing and preserving the space between childhood and adulthood. There is ample evidence that shows

Chapter VI: Hip-Hop and Masculinity

young people have forged their own rites of passage (Sande, 2002). Hip-hop as a liminal rite of passage will be the focus of this chapter.

Hip-hop functions as a liminal rite of passage because hip-hop is praxis, it requires participation. One does not merely listen to hip-hop, one lives it (KRS-One, 1995). It is almost impossible to be a fan of hip-hop and not actively support it and personalize it. Intentionally or not, either by buying an album, CD, MP3 download, or purchasing and wearing hip-hop apparel, you take part in hip-hop culture. Even those who are past the age of adolescence still engage in the culture of hip-hop and serve as "keepers-of-the guard" or give advice to others about the true essence of hip-hop and how to keep it real. These watchdogs therefore remain active in the ritual of hip-hop, serving as councils of elders by helping others to remember the past and complete the circle between initiates and veterans.

Break-dancers use physical comedy, drama, and spectacle in their performances. The D-jay pays respect to former enclave members by balancing old school music with the latest music to forge new audio collages. In these face-offs, the MC competes against other rappers for style and delivery using tropes and alliteration, creating reality and identity as they perform. In addition, the attire of the audience, the performers, and the fliers that announced the event are influenced by the visual medium of hip-hop graffiti. Leaving the circle serves as the symbolic integration back into society and functions as the third and final rite of passage.

As long as the participants perform within culturally approved norms, win or lose, the audience accepts their contribution to the ritual. Even those who are past their prime for break-dancing or feel too old to take part in MCing, Djaying or performing acts of graffiti are given special places of honor within the hip-hop community. They are watchdogs of tradition and ensure new trends are conducted in the spirit and identity of the past, signaled with a nod of the head that points out the participants are "keeping it real."

In contrast to social science communication and anthropological accounts that have researched adolescent delinquency, negative effects of hip-hop, and how rites of passage strengthen society, this chapter features critical points of interest from the individuals taking part in the rites of passage. In other words, instead of looking at hip-hop from the outside, this chapter includes accounts from the global hip-hop community who experience it, those who are on the inside. Hip-hop frames a space for adolescent artistic expression (Flores, 2002), often brought about by feelings of frustration. In the insiders' accounts that follow, hip-hop listeners detail feelings of marginalization, vulnerability, cultural and ethnic pride as well as self-realization, told in the vivid and expressive vernacular of their point of view. These feelings mirror van Gennep's second and transitional stage of his rites of passage theory, limen. To explicate the interconnected and interrelated ideas of global adolescent liminal rites of passage, a brief knowledge of hip-hop is necessary.

Brief History of Hip-Hop

Hip-hop was created in the New York borough of the Bronx in the 1970s by young, disenfranchised American youth of African American, Latino American, Caribbean American, Irish American, Italian American, and Jewish American ethnicity. As well as belonging to diverse cultural and ethnic backgrounds, this group of youths had something else in common: They found themselves culturally ostracized by the larger ethnic group, those of mainly White Anglo-Saxon Protestant descent. Preserving ethnic identity was important for self-assistance and to protect resources. During the 1970s, a gang truce that included many of New York's adolescents was in place. A local D-jay named Afrika Bambaattaa, along with Kool DJ Herc and Grandmaster Flash came up with the idea to "channel the anger of young people in the south Bronx away from gang fighting and into music, dance, and graffiti" (Nelson, 2004, p. 45). These young men, many of whom were former gang members crafted names to represent a group identity as well their neighborhoods ("hoods") with names like the Rock Steady Crew, Bronx City Bombers and Zulu Nation. For those adolescents that were "denied opportunity for more formal music training and access to instruments due to Reagan-era budget cuts in education and school music programs, turntables became instruments and lyrical acrobats became a cultural outlet" (Lusane, 2004, p. 351). Because of a lack of funding for music and after-school programs in the 1970s, in many ways society itself created the need for hip-hop.

Most of the creators and founders of hip-hop were male, and most of them were minorities. Facing a lack of economic and educational opportunities, these early participants and followers of hip-hop felt a fundamental challenge to their manhood. They felt abandoned, betrayed, alienated, and disrespected by society (Payne, 2006). Hip-hop was and is largely influenced by African American males, and that includes the 70% of Black children that are born to single mothers (Morgan, 1999). Left without a father in the home, these young men are expected to model their own identity "through communal culture, stand up against all prevailing threats, garner respect, remain loyal to immediate family, friends, and community, and provide by any means necessary for self and immediate family" (Payne, 2006, p. 295). For many African American adolescents, there is no real definition of manhood or models to follow, so for many Black males what it means to be

Chapter VI: Hip-Hop and Masculinity

male has to be self-modeled, often with hypermasculine language and posturing. The role of brotherhood in hip-hop culture is often symbolically replaced with close friends that serve as family.

This history of hip-hop that imploded within New York City and then exploded to the rest of America and the world, highlights repeating themes found in global hip-hop culture. Disenfranchisement, feelings of alienation, and a search for identity are common themes for adolescents not only in America but all over the world. Now that a background has been established, the liminal transition of hip-hop can be discussed.

Analysis

American Hip-Hop

Hip-hop can be effectively divided and analyzed into four distinct "families" or genres: graffiti, b-boying, D-jaying, and rap. In an article by Bonz Malone for *Source Magazine*, hip-hop originator and innovator Richie Colon, better known as Crazy Legs, describes the four elements or "children" of hip-hop: "Graffiti is the Black Sheep. B-boying is the bastard child of hip-hop. D-Jaying is the loyal child who always does what it is told. Rap is the spoiled brat who is actually the youngest of the four" (Malone, 2003, p. 132). Hip-hop is also further defined by "old-skool" for the originators and "new-skool" for performers who are non-traditionalists (Mitchell, 1998). I take these self-defined elements of hip-hop, explained in terms of family, children, and learning, as indicative of hip-hop's interconnected relationship to adolescence.

It is important to note that ritual functions as a reciprocal action that marks both an individual passage as well as a collective journey. An individual temporally has to separate from the group to examine one's place in society, just as ritual in turn "creates, sustains and perpetuates social meaning" (Draper, 2003, p. 75) for the group. African Americans are constantly held in transitional discursive thresholds, owing an identity that is in some ways created by mainstream America as they simultaneously influence it. Both contaminated and contained, Blacks hold liminal spaces, moving along a continuum toward a more acceptable status (Entman & Rojecki, 2000). How hip-hop functions as a liminal rite of passage will start as an exegesis of an overarching African American cultural theme that features life-and-death issues or as it is known in hip-hop culture, from the cradle to the grave.

> Somebody wake me I'm dreaming, I started as a seed the semen, swimming upstream, planted in the womb while screaming on the top was my pops, my momma hollering stop, from a single drop, this is what they got? (2 Pac, 1999, track 2)

The Art of Being Cool

In this verse 2 Pak—*Tupac Shakur*—arguably the world's most famous rapper, verbally illustrates a compelling, interrelated story of frustration for those who feel they are victims of institutional social structures that they did not create. Tupac is consistently crossing the fluid, liminal boundary between self-awareness and collective consciousness. On one side, he is detailing an event that happened before he was even born, while on the other side, he is self-aware enough to realize his own oppression but unable to change the social system that created it. From his conception portrayed as a rape, to his passage from his mother's womb, Tupac is signifying the separation stage in a rite of passage. It is an allegory of the rape of Mother Africa and theft of her sons, forcibly transported (separated from Africa) to another land commonly referred to as the Middle Passage. Tupac's ability to make inner-city life real and available to the masses even from the grave is one of the key reasons for rumors that he is still alive. His lyrics make it seem as if he has broken the threshold of death, is still in the present and aware of what is happening now. In truth, he is more celebrated in death, for he is often described as someone who died for the struggle. Respect for former members who have passed on is common in the hip-hop culture as well as other cultures. Remembering Tupac as someone who struggled and died for the cause of truth and authenticity is a way to pay respect to the past.

In Black Power circles, people refer to "the struggle" as a political movement, but Tupac refers to the struggle as just the fight to survive every day. His is the struggle to be Black, the struggle of not having a voice and the struggle of not having control of your community, and it is Tupac's recounting of this which makes him so popular after his death.

> Pistol whippin these simps, for bein petrified and lame. Disrespectin the game, prayin for punishment and pain. Goin insane, never die, live eternal, who shall I fear? Don't shed a tear for me nigga I ain't happy hear. I hope they bury me and send me to my rest. Headlines reading murdered to death, my last breath. (2 Pac, 1998, track 2)

Of him, Michael Eric Dyson said:

> Tupac had an instinctive ability to make the most wretched members of society, what he calls thug niggaz, seem real, palpable, human and in this sense I see a special kind of folk heroic creation. (Dyson, 2004, p. 76)

Tupac makes violent aggression not only rational but necessary for survival for young Black males to be taken seriously. The theme that a rapper must be ready and able to fight to the

Chapter VI: Hip-Hop and Masculinity

death for his close contacts crew, or urban tribe, is a common theme in hip-hop. Rakim, another immensely popular rapper worldwide says:

> I take seven MCs put 'em in a line, and add seven more brothers who think they can rhyme. Well it'll take seven more before I go for mine, and that's 21 MCs ate up at the same time. (Rakim, 1996, track 3)

This passage is an allegorical tribute to a sharpshooter who lines up and eliminates his targets, and like so much of hip-hop it is strongly associated with violence. But it is likely that its dialect and appeal are based more on allusions to aggression and survival in an urban jungle than actual acts of violence.

Latin American Hip-Hop

From its start, Latin hip-hop has paralleled African American hip-hop. For example, Latin American hip-hop is so replete with gang imagery that it often embodies the same lyrical tropes centering on violence and sexual conquest. Except for its occasional reference to Latino culture (such as a mention below of Aztec warriors) and use of Spanish words like *varrio* for ghetto and *vato* for homeboy, often Latin hip-hop is indistinguishable from African American hip-hop. The first Latino to have a gold single was a Cuban American known as MC Mellow Man Ace whose best selling song was his 1990 release *Mentirosa* (Flores, 2000). MC Kid Frost, a Chicano from Chicago released his album *Hispanic Causing Panic* in the same year.

> *Quevo, Aqui'stoy* (I'm MC Kid Frost). *Yo estoy* (I am in charge). My *carbon* is the big boss. *My cuete* (gun) is loaded. It's full of *balas* (bullets). I'll put it in your face. And you won't say *nada* (nothing). *Vatos, cholos* (homeboys), call us what you will. You say we are assassins. Train ourselves to kill. It's in our blood to be an Aztec warrior. Go to any extreme. And hold no barriers. Chicano and I'm Brown and proud. Want this *chingaso* (verbal beat down)? *Si mon,* I said let's get down. (Kid Frost, 1994, side A)

Clearly, MC Kid Frost is vacillating between the metaphor of physical use of force and lyrical forcefulness to break down aural barriers. To him and other Latin bilingual speakers, weapons-related firepower is analogous to the lyrical firepower of expression. This reinforces the lyrical potency of the language of hip-hop. Only until recently with the explosion of reggaetone, Spanish rap over reggae rhythms and Latin dance music, has Latin hip-hop been separated from African American hip-hop.

German Hip-Hop

Hip-hop's focus on violence highlights its struggle based in part on society's demands of self-protection for masculinity and maleness. It has been said that "Since both manhood and honor cannot be gained but only lost, a permanent readiness to fight is required" (Tertilt, 1996, p. 175). One might naturally assume the quote is taken from an article about African American hip-hop or Latin hip-hop; instead, it comes from the book *Turkish Power Boys* (Tertilt, 1996). It would also be logical to assume that the title refers to young adolescents of Turkish descent. Instead, *Turkish Power Boys* alludes to the romanticized ideology among the many youth who are immigrants, living in Germany and having both Turkish and Dutch-German heritage. German-language rap has come to signify the voice of second generation immigrants including the Turks, who are trying to integrate into German society (Bennett, 2000).

The first German rap record was released in 1988 by the West Berlin group Rock Da Most. By 1994, every 10th citizen of the Federal Republic of Germany (FRG) was foreign; in addition to Turks, the country was comprised of Italian, Greek, Yugoslavian, and Polish immigrants. The largest immigrant population in the FRG is Turkish. Just a year previous, in 1993, a rap group named the Cartel was targeted toward one million Turkish adolescents in FRG.

A CD cover design for the Cartel was carefully crafted with the "C" drawn as a crescent. This ornamental "C" was reminiscent of the Turkish national flag and Islam (Elfein, 1998). African American rappers such as Rakim and Ice Cube and U. S. rap groups such as NWA, often acknowledge Islamic inspiration in their lyrical material. However, in FRG hip-hop, one distinction is made. German/Turkish identity is in transition, still being created discursively. It is still being created by the originators who are striving for an identity in Germany. In other words, they are performing in the liminal threshold between what is expected of Germans and Turks who share aspects of each other. African Americans and Turkish Germans have this undefined limbo in common, trying to establish what should be accepted from the dominant culture while describing what is taboo and to be shunned to preserve a distinct ethnic identity.

Chapter VI: Hip-Hop and Masculinity

The language used in FRG rap is called *Kanak Sprak*—or "nigger speak." The FRG hip-hop enthusiasts see themselves as "White Niggas" because they believe they are similar to African Americans (Elfein, 1998). They live in a state of confusion, constantly having to reinvent themselves with positive descriptors to counter the negatives ones handed to them. The noise or dissonance they create is part of a worldwide community of adolescents that exchanges ideas through hip-hop. This community includes all those who are powerless in their communities. As Elfein points out, never before in the history of FRG popular music have adolescent immigrants produced a culture separate and distinct from that of their parents (1998). Identity discourses are notorious for providing audiences for competition and creating national and cultural identity.

Japanese Hip-Hop

The term "Oriental hip-hop" is not hip-hop from Asia. It was created in West Germany and contains an amalgamation of Turkish Arabesque, FRG Pop Muzik and African American influences. However, parts of Asia have a distinct hip-hop culture, and adolescent participants are struggling with ethnic identity as much as the adolescents in FRG.

In Japan, adolescents who embrace African American hip-hop are called Jiggers. Some members of the Japanese hip-hop community habitually visit tanning salons to darken their skin, and some wear their hair in dreadlocks and afros. This appropriated style is called *Burapan* (Condry, 2007). It combines two Japanese words *pansuke* and *burakku*—prostitute and black respectively. Other Japanese pop groups like the Gosperats further push the envelope of experimental ethnicity by wearing blackface during their performances. Behavior like this has caused resentment among Africans and African Americans as well as other Japanese. A popular Japanese rapper Banana Ice, for example, criticizes other Japanese who mimic other cultures and ignore the history and pride of their own. For those like Banana Ice who disagree with the use of minstrel-style black face used by Japanese who mimic African Americans, introspection begs the question: What is the difference between the African Americans who call themselves the Asian name Wu-Tang Clan and the African Americans who created and then supported the Asian television cartoon *Buddha Samurai?*

In the United States, slavery is viewed as the paramount theme on discussions of racism. In Japan, racism centers on World War II. Just as Nazi Germany conducted the holocaust of the Jews and tried to dominate the world, Japan attempted to ally itself with other Asians against European oppression intent on placing itself at the forefront of a greater East Asia with Japan as the head. Consequently because of its embarrassing context, Japanese textbooks have told a watered-down story of World War II that diminishes the fervent love of the rising sun on the Japanese flag that occurred before the end of the war. In modern Japanese schools, children are taught to think of themselves as grandchildren of the devil with little attention paid to positive aspects of Japanese identity (Condry, 2007, p. 663). In many ways rappers like Banana Ice are asking Japanese hip-hop listeners to reexamine what it means to be Japanese.

Southeast Asian Hip-Hop

Hip-hop also serves as a playground in which to experiment and discuss what it means to be South Asian. In fact, "Hip-Hop provides individuals with a vocabulary for racial consciousness and tools for the expression of racial identities" for many South Asians (Sharma, 2005, p. 19). One fitting example of South Asians who use hip-hop to express and examine issues of identity is Steven Kapur, better known as Apache Indian. Kapur's first album *No Reservation*, was released in 1993 and at the time he was paid one of the largest recording contracts for a debut album by an non-White artist. This is significant because Steve was born in Birmingham, England, is of South Asian descent and uses a Native American Indian moniker.

With his name Apache, Steve connects many different aspects of nationality and ethnicity in a very unique way. But Steve is not alone in the way South Asians use hip-hop to experiment with identity. Below, Ryan Gujurati, Indian and hip-hop journalist tells how hip-hop, in this case specifically African American-influenced hip-hop, created ethnic space for him.

> I think hip hop's anti-establishment sensibilities resonated with the general feeling I felt about me—reveling in being different and "un-mainstream." Hip-hop at that time was really political, whether it was obvious (Public Enemy) or not (De La Soul). It was through [Black culture] that I then discovered my own politics. I started to gain pride in being both Indian and contrarian. I learned a lot about the Black experience and saw that as the defining framework for ANY race discussions in America. (Ryan in Nitasha, Sharma, 2005, p. 13)

Chapter VI: Hip-Hop and Masculinity

Although South Asian music and the particular ethnic flavor that it brings has been in the United States for years—even before MC Apache Indian—it was not until recently that it became popular in to American hip-hop audiences. In 2002, R&B artist Truth Hurts released a single entitled *Addictive* on Aftermath Records that featured a chorus with a 20-year-old Hindu song by East Indian artist Laa Mangheshkar (Sharma, 2005). Shortly afterward, also in 2002, hip-hop rappers Eric Sermon and Redman sampled another Hindu song *React* on J Records. By 2003, American hip-hop fans were well acquainted with South Asian music with the release of three commercially successful and heavily Indian influenced *Thoia Thong* by R. Kelly, *Get Yr Freak On*, by Missy Elliot, and Jay Z's re-mix of Punjabi MC's *Mundian to Bach Ke—Beware of the Boys*. Southeast Asian hip-hop is heavily influenced by Bhangra, a style of music and dance from the Punjab region in India (Sanjay, in Sharma, 1996). Punjab has a history of both political and social upheaval that influences South Asian cultural ideology. In the lyrics to "The Middle Passage" by the San Francisco hip-hop duo Himalayan Project, they express South Asian political and ethnic attitudes toward the 1964 Civil Rights Act signed by President Lyndon Johnson and the enactment of the Immigration and Nationality Act of 1965:

> What's goin' on America, it's your least favorite son, you know the one some beast mixed with East Indian rum. Hemmed, condemned to rent slum tents in dense settlements. See my melanin's akin to a felon's sins in this civilization. Where dead presidents replacing the Gods you're praising, Jesus? Nah, it's just g's, churches is worthless, it's a circus, clowning around ain't where the work is. I breathe the oxygen, cough a lung, sit and think for my people hope my freedom songs get sung. (The Himalayan Project, 2003)

The Immigration and Nationality Act of 1965 gave preferential immigration rights to highly skilled, English-speaking and English–educated, professional, middle and upper caste Indians. As a result, the South Asian community is one of the fastest growing, highly educated and most affluent in North America (Maira, 2002).

Despite the common misconception that Asians are the perfect minority, in both Japan and South Asia, Asians deal with ethnic and cultural identity issues as much as any other place. Both Japanese hip-hop and South Asian hip-hop provide a space to discuss inter-ethnic issues.

The Art of Being Cool

Australian Hip-Hop

Australian identity is based more on otherness (Mitchell, 1998) than nationality. Australia adolescent minorities include Chinese, Korean, South American, and Aboriginals. Australian rap is inclusive of many different languages and includes lyrics recited in Jamaican Reggae accents, French, and Spanish.

The first collection of Australian rap was released on Virgin Records in 1988 and consisted of compilations under one title *Down Under by Law* without widespread success. The only Australian rap album that did make a noticeable impact in the mid-1990s was Sound Unlimited's *A Postcard from the Edge of the Under-side*, and the only Australian rap album to be released on a major label was Def Wish Cast's *Knights of the Underground Table* (Mitchell, 1999). Both groups are from the suburbs of Sydney in Western Australia, with large populations of Greek Italian, Lebanese, and Vietnamese youth. While these ethnically dense populations and enclaves may not have the same types of ghettos as exist in American inner cities, they have suburbs that mirror the same conditions (Powell, 1994). Whether in the inner city or the suburbs, Australian adolescents feel separated from society and use hip-hop as a subculture to which they can belong. In terms of Australian inner cities and suburbs and the way in which adolescents use these spaces to rehearse hip-hop, this chapter can do no better than to quote an important study by Tony Mitchell:

> There are 10 sub-cultural aspects of the Australian city of Sydney that hip-hop fans actively participate and recognize: 1. Seclusion of where hip-hop is performed and separated from mainstream media outlets. 2. Hip-hop crews stress independence and self reliability by promoting and producing their music on their own without record company conglomerates. 3. An overwhelming resistance to commercialization. 4. Idealization that graffiti is an illegal activity and not a cultural art form. 5. Hip-hop is male dominated in Sydney. 6. Sydney hip-hop is heavily influenced by American hip-hop. 7. Sydney hip-hop has an emphasis in keeping it real and authentic. 8. There is a strong attachment to identifiers of places of origin, neighborhood, family, community and ethnic group identity through crews. 9. It incorporates all of the four elements of hip-hop graffiti, B-boying, D-jaying and Mc-ing. 10. Sydney hip-hop uses skill-based hierarchies, values and rules (Mitchell, 2003)

Chapter VI: Hip-Hop and Masculinity

In addition to the praxis of the 10 aspects of Australian hip-hop and its obvious relationship to rites of passage, there are also discursive elements of its specific brand of hip-hop (Mitchell, 2003). One example is Sound Unlimited's song "Unity" that encourages the Australian homogenous style of expression:

> Here we go! Get ready for some info; ya wanna know how far my posse can grow? Worldwide! All my brothers are colorblind Breakin' down the barriers of culture and tribe comin' live! Why can't you stop and see All we need is unity! (Rosano, Martinez, MC Kode Blue, DJ BTL, 1991)

Here, Sound Unlimited clearly advances the idea that hip-hop is a color-blind medium in which to establish cultural, ethnic, religious, and social unity. This concept steps away from the American point of view of hip-hop as purely an African American cultural art form. Australian hip-hop has a history of advancing hip-hop as part of a global culture unifying all adolescents who need a medium in which to express themselves within America and without.

East African Hip-Hop

Despite the fact that the East African country of Tanzania is one of the poorest places in the world, it has still found a way to develop contemporary ways to market and export its brand of hip-hop through CDs with musical content that express the problems, worries, and dreams of their generation and location (Casco, 2006). Tanzanian rappers are known as *maemesi*—MCs—and they are marketed in Kenya, Uganda, Europe, and as far away as North America. For many Tanzanian adolescents, hip-hop serves the same social function of the traditional Swahili poets who used to express people's trials and tribulations along its coast. The former Swahili poets believed that their words should contribute positive messages to the community through sophisticated, prosodic rules and an elegant use of the language (Middleton, 1992).

Tanzanian hip-hop first became popular during the 1980s in the port of Dar es Salaam, where goods are shipped and received from all over the world. The affluence lifestyle brought about by the money and apparel of the locals in this port has given Tanzanian adolescents something to admire and copy. In 1990 at the New Africa Hotel and the Kilimanjaro Poolside, a rapper named Saleh Jabir translated for the first time English language rap into Swahili language rap without losing meaning (Gesthuizen, 2002b). Later, rappers inserted political and socially conscious lyrics (Casco, 2006), also performed in Swahili.

Tanzanian hip-hop has two categories. The first comprises "old-skool" members, who are characterized by performers who detail the public hostility toward their music, in conjunction with their lack of opportunities, poor audio equipment, and a limited commercial market in which to sell their product. The second category comprises "new-skool" members, who are marked by the almost unheard of institutionally and socially approved inclusion of rap as a musical category by BASTA, the Tanzanian Arts Council Baraza ya Sanii ya Tansania (Casco, 2006). The debate over the positive and negative aspects of hip-hop in Tanzania mirrors the same discussion about hip-hop all over the world, as many "old-skool" artists are unhappy about how "new-skool" artists are degrading the authenticity of hip-hop—in this instance, by not keeping it real and only talking about the sunny side of life (Cambridge, 2003). Despite the "old-skool/new-skool" division, Tanzanian rappers like Professor Jay say that hip-hop is the best medium in which to expose Tanzanian social disparities (Casco, 2006).

This common sentiment, combined with the fact that Dar es Salaam is a hub of international activity, has contributed to the popularity of Tanzanian-style hip-hop. Currently BASTA encourages lyrics that discuss social problems such as AIDS, sexual abuse, and lack of education (Gesthuizen, 2002a). This awareness of hip-hop's social functionality mirrors earlier, 16th century Muslim scholars' views: contemporary literary forms were useful tools to teach social tenets such as Islam to younger generations (Knappert, 1979). For the most part, Tanzanian rappers tend not to focus on the violent aspects of hip-hop and instead concentrate on reality-based messages of East Africa told in their native language of Swahili, which is largely responsible for its widespread popularity (Perullo, 2005). In fact, in a 2003 poll, 41% of Tanzanians voted that the most important thing in hip-hop is the content and quality of the Swahili lyrics and *mashairi*—the verses of the music (Cambridge, 2003).

Mashairi verses are sometimes included in public festivities called *mashindano*—competitions in which contenders have to compose rhymes replying to what their opponents previously said (Biersteker, 1996; Biersteker & Shariff, 1995). These competitions, similar in form and fashion to the American hip-hop circle face-off are all about the *mtindo*—style of the lyrics of the *maemesi*, skill of the D-jays, and the influence from the traditional local dancers, the *ngoma* (Casco, 2006). This is all done with *Bongo Flava*—hip-hop from and influenced by Dar es Salaam's inhabitants, and it incorporates R&B, rumba, taarab, and

Chapter VI: Hip-Hop and Masculinity

lingla styles of music. Lyrics of Bongo Flava, such as the ones performed by Mr. II often touch on police abuse, unemployment, and the plight of girls who feel that they have to prostitute themselves just for survival (Casco, 2006).

Tanzanian hip-hop can be summed up in one word: rights (*haki*). This theme involves the almost nonexistent rights for adolescents in Tanzania and their fight to achieve equity, as eloquently expressed by Mr. II who also uses the name Sugu:

> *Wabongo mnataka nini?* (What do people of Dar es Salaam want?)
>
> *Haki, herufi zake chache sana neon.* (Rights! Very few letters for the word
>
> *haki.*)
>
> *Haikuiazimu kushika bunduki, haki!* (It must not be necessary to hold a rifle to
>
> get our rights.) (Mr. II, 2002, track 1)

Bongo flava does not represent all of East African hip-hop. On the contrary, in neighboring Kenya, hip-hop has been embraced by red-robed Masai warriors, and they have their own brand of hip-hop that is different and apart from Tanzania (Hudson, 2004). In fact, one Kenyan rap group X Plastaz, feels that they are more political than their Tanzanian counterparts (Thompson, 2008). The internationally famous hip-hop crew X Plastaz was formed in 1995 and they are accredited with linking hip-hop and Masai chanting (Gesthuizen, 2002). They also stress authenticity by performing in Masai clothing and promote themselves using Masai imagery (Thompson, 2008). However, X Plastaz has come under criticism stemming from the fact that only one of the members is Masai, leading to opinions that they are exploiting Masai warriors for their own financial gains. This is despite the fact that they refuse to pay bribes to local D-jays to play their music (Thompson, 2008). In this regard at least, X Plastaz is keeping it real.

Conclusion

This chapter steps away from previous research that has focused on adolescent delinquency and the negative effects of hip-hop. It explored the idea that hip-hop is often thought of as Black and cool but is actually embraced as a form of masculinity by males all over the globe. With firsthand accounts and a literature review, this chapter has shown how hip-hop has unified adolescents all over the globe by providing opportunities for disenfranchised youth to rehearse and explore ideas about race, culture, and ethnicity;

The Art of Being Cool

space to present their imaginative literal and symbolic ideas; and a forum for these practices to be heard and legitimized. This chapter also looked at adolescence and hip-hop as a rite of passage for a modern global village. Sources were taken from African American, Latin American, Turkish German, Japanese, South Asian, Australian, and East African forms of hip-hop. It is hoped that this chapter will prompt further and continuous research on regions that practice the art of hip-hop.

With the help of modern media, hip-hop and technology have brought today's youth together, centering them on cultural unifiers where ideas about ethnic identity, language, clothing, and behavior are reformed and redistributed in different ways. Hip-hop has done this despite barriers of race, language, and religion. Since the definition of being an adolescent involves a transition between childhood and adulthood, hip-hop fits the requirement of a rite of passage. A rite of passage is ideally a ritual that transmits cultural expectations from one generation to another. The influential scholar Cornel West tells us that hip-hop exorcises "the demons of cultural amnesia" (West in Dyson, 2004, p. 66). However, going one step further, hip-hop functions as a liminal rite of passage because hip-hop is praxis; it requires participation and separation from what is considered mainstream. In that regard, we can view hip-hop as a ritualistic transmission of self-identity and -expression by those who perform it. One does not merely listen to hip-hop; a true hip-hop fan lives it.

References

Alexander, B. C. (March, 1991). Correcting misinterpretations of Turner's theory: An African-American Pentecostal illustration. *Journal for the Scientific Study of Religion, 30*(1), 26-44.

Alford, K. A. (2003). Cultural themes in rites of passage: Voices of young African American males. *Journal of African American Studies, 7*(1), 3-26.

Aufderheide, P. (Winter, 1986). Music videos: The look of the sound. *Journal of Communication, 36*(1), 57-78.

Baumeister, R. F., & Leary, M. R. (May, 1995). The need to belong: Desire for interpersonal attachments as a fundamental human motivation. *Psychological Bulletin, 117*(3), 497–529.

Bennett, A. (2000). Hip-hop culture as a local construct in two European cities. In *Popular music and youth culture,* pp. 133-165. New York: Palgrave.

Bendix, L. (1970). *International encyclopedia of social sciences, volumes 1-17:* A review. *Psychoanalytic Quarterly, 39,* 153-155.

Biersteker, A. (1996). Kujibizana. *Questions of language and lower in nineteenth- and twentieth-century poetry in Kiswahili.* East Lansing, MI: Michigan State University Press (African Series, 4).

Biersteker, A., & Shariff, I. N. (Eds.). (1995) *Mashairi ya vita vya Kuduhu (Poem of the Kuduhu War).* East Lansing, MI: Michigan State University Press (African Historical Sources, 7).

Big Pun. (1998). Still not a player. *Capital punishment.* New York: Loud Records.

Blimankrantz, D., & Gavazzi, S. (1993). Guiding transitional events for children and adolescents through a modern day rite of passage. *Journal of Primary Prevention, 13*(3), 199-212.

Bloch, H., & Niederhoffer, A. (1958). *The gang: A study of adolescent behavior.* New York: Philosophical Library.

Brewer, M. B. (1991). The social self: On being the same and different at the same time. *Personality and Social Psychology Bulletin, 17*, 475-482.

Cambridge, E. (2003). Bongo Flava (still) hidden "underground" rap from Morogoro, Tanzania. *Vienna Journal of African Studies, 5*(3), 72–93.

Casco, J. A. S. (2006). The language of the young people: Rap, urban culture and protest in Tanzania. *Journal of Asian & African Studies, 41*(3), 229-248.

Condry, I. (2007). Yellow b-boys, Black culture, and hip-hop in Japan: Toward a transnational cultural politics of race. *Duke University Press Positions, 15*(3), 637-671.

Draper, J. (March, 2002). Men's passage to fatherhood: an analysis of the contemporary relevance of transition theory. *Nursing Inquiry, 10*(1), 66-78.

Dyson, M. (2004). *The Michael Eric Dyson reader.* New York: Basic Civitas Books.

Edelman, M. W. (1995). United we stand: A common vision. *Claiming Children, 1*, 6-12.

Elfein, D. (1998). From Krauts with attitudes to Turks with attitudes: Some aspects of hip-hop history in Germany. *Popular Music, 17*(3), 255-265.

Entman, R., & Rojecki, A. (2000). *The Black image in the White mind: Media and race in America.* Chicago: University of Chicago Press.

Epstein, J., Pratto, D., & Skipper, J. (1990). Teenagers, behavioral problems, and preferences for heavy metal and rap music: A case of a Southern middle school. *Deviant Behavior, 11*, 381-394.

Flores, J. (2002). *From bomba to hip-hop: Puerto Rican culture and Latino identity. Ethnomusicology, 46*(2), 334-336.

Gerbner, G., Gross, L., Morgan, M., & Signorielli, N. (1986). Living with television: The dynamics of the cultivation process. In J. Bryant, & D. Zillman (Eds.), *Perspectives on media effects* (pp. 17-40). Hilldale, NJ: Lawrence Erlbaum Associates.

Gesthuizen, T. (2002a). Hip-hop in Tanzania. Available at http://www.niza.nl/Gesthuizen, T. (2002b). Saleh J: Tanzanian pioneer. Available at http://www.african hiphop.com/

Chapter VI: Hip-Hop and Masculinity

Hansen, C. (1995). Predicting cognitive and behavioral effects of gansta rap. *Basic and Applied Social Psychology, 16,* 43-52.

Hebdige, D. (1979). *Subculture: The meaning of style.* London: Methuen.

The Himalayan Project. (2002). The middle passage. *The Middle Passage.* [CD]. San Francisco: CD Baby.

Hofferth, S. L., Pleck, J. H., Stueve, J. L., Bianchi, S., & Sayer, L. (2002). The demography of fathers: What fathers do. In C. Tamis-LeMonda & N. Cabrera (Eds.), *Handbook of father involvement: Multidisciplinary perspectives* (pp. 63–90). Mahwah, NJ: Erlbaum.

Hudson, M. (October 30, 2004). Reviews: Music [Review of global hip-hop]. *Daily Telegraph.*

Jones, R. (Ed.). (2004). *Black psychology* (4th ed). Hampton, VA: Cobb and Henry.

Jung, C. G. (1966). *The spirit in man, art, and literature.* New York: Pantheon.

Katz, J., & Earp, J. (1999). *Tough guise violence: Media and the crisis in masculinity* [video recording]. Northampton, MA: Media Education Foundation.

Kid Frost (1994). *Terminator* [Rough cut, 12"]. Miami: Electro Beat.

King, V., Harris, K. M., & Heard, H. E. (2004). Racial and ethnic diversity in nonresident father involvement. *Journal of Marriage and Family, 66,* 1-21.

Knappert, J. (1979). *Four centuries of Swahili verse: A literary history and anthology.* London: Heinemann Educational Books.

KRS-One. (1995). *The Source Magazine.* New York: L. Londell McMillan.

Lerman, R., & Sorenson, E. (2000). Father involvement with their nonmarital children. *Marriage and Family Review, 29*(2-3), 137-158.

Lusane, C. (2004). Rap, race and politics. In M. Forman & M. A. Neal (Eds.), *That's the joint! The hip-hop studies reader* (pp. 351-362). New York: Routledge.

Maddern, E. (1990). What is it fifteen-year-olds need? Notes on developing initiations appropriate to our times. *Adventure Education, 17*(1), 29-32.

Maffesoli, M. (1996). *The time of the tribes: The decline of individualism in mass society.* London: Sage Publications.

Malone, B. (2003). Chief rocka. *The Source Magazine: The Magazine of Hip-Hop Music,Culture, Politics (15th anniversary jumpoff), 167,* 130-133.

Males, M. A. (1999). *Framing youth: 10 myths about the next generation* (1st ed.). Monroe, ME: Common Courage Press.

Maira, S. (2002). *Desi's in the house: Indian American youth culture in New York City.* Philadelphia: Temple University Press.

McGuire, W., McGuire, C., Child, P., & Fujioka, T. (1978). Salience of ethnicity in the spontaneous self-concept as a function of one's ethnic distinctiveness in the social environment. *Journal of Personality and Social Psychology, 36*(5), 511-520.

McLuhan, M. (1962). *The Gutenberg galaxy: The making of typographic man.* Toronto: University of Toronto Press.

McKenry, P., Everett, J., Ramseur, H., & Carter, C. (1989). Research on Black adolescents: A legacy of cultural bias. *Journal of Adolescent Research, 4,* 254-64.

Middleton, J. (1992). *The world of the Swahili: An African mercantile civilization.* New Haven, CT: Yale University Press.

Mitchell, T. (1998). *Australian Hip-Hop as a "Glocal" Subculture.* Paper presented at Urban Expressions conference, Ultimo series. Sydney: University of Technology.

Mitchell, T. (1999). Another root: Australian hip-hop as a "global" subculture. *The Ultimo Series Seminar Review, 5,* 126-141.

Mitchell, T. (2003). Australian hip-hop as a subculture. *Youth Studies Australia, (22)*2.

Morgan, J. (1999). *When chicken-heads come home to roost: A hip-hop feminist breaks it down.* New York: Touchstone.

Mr. II. (2002). Haki: East coast team. *Itikadi* [CD]. Dar es Salaam, Tanzania: G.M.C. Records.

Nas & Thompson, C. (2002). One mic. *Stillmatic.* New York: Ill Will Records, Columbia.

Nelson, G. (2004). Hip-hop's founding fathers speak the truth. In M. Forman & M. A. Neal (Eds.), *That's the joint! The hip-hop studies reader* (pp. 45-55). New York: Routledge.

Notorius B.I.G. (1994). Things done changed. *Ready to die.* New York: Puff Daddy Records.

Papachristos, A. (1998). The death of telemachus: Street gangs and the decline of modern rites of passage. *Journal of Gang Research, 5*(4), 35-44.

Payne, D., & Cornwell, B. (2007). Reconsidering peer influences on delinquency: Do less proximate contacts matter? *Journal of Quantitative Criminology, 23*(2), 127-149.

Payne, Y. (2006). A gangster and a gentleman: How street life-oriented, U.S.-born African men negotiate issues of survival in relation to their masculinity. *Men and Masculinities, 8,* 288-297.

Powell, D. (1994). *Out west: Perceptions of Sydney's Western suburbs.* Sydney, Australia: Allen and Unwin.

Perullo, A. (forthcoming). "Here's a little something local": An early history of hip-hop in Dar es Salaam, Tanzania, 1984–1997. In J. Brennan, A. Burton, & Y. Lawi (Eds.), *Dar es Salaam: The history of an emerging East African metropolis.* Dar es Salaam: Mikuki na Nyota Publishers and British Institute in East Africa.

Rakim. (1996). My melody. *Paid in full: Eric B. and Rakim* [CD]. New York: Fourth & Bway.

Rakim. (1999). When I b on the mic. *The master.* New York: Universal Records.

Rogers, E. M. (1962). Diffusion of innovations. New York: Free Press.

Rosano, Martinez, T., MC Kode Blue, & DJ BTL. (1991). Unity. *Unity: Sound Unlimited* [LP]. Sydney: CBS Records Australia.

Sande, A. (2002). Intoxication and rite of passage to adulthood in Norway. **Contemporary Drug Problems, 29,** part 2, 277-304.

Schwartz, T. (1972). Review of Turner's *The ritual process. American Anthropologist, 74*, 904–08.

Sharma, N. (2005). *Musical Crossings: Identity Formations of Second-Generation South Asian American Hip-Hop Artists.* Institute for the Study of Social Change, ISSC Fellows Working Papers.

Sharma, S. (1996). Noisy Asians or "Asian noise"? In S. Sharma, J. Hutnyk, & A. Sharma (Eds.), *Disorienting rhythms: The politics of the new Asian dance music* (pp. 32-57). London: Zed Books.

Steinberg, L. (1993). *Adolescence* (3rd ed.). New York: McGraw-Hill.

2 Pac. (1998). If I die tonight. *Me against the world* [AC]. New York: Jive Records.

2 Pac. (1999). Still I rise. *Still I rise* [CD]. Los Angeles: Interscope Records.

Tarry, H., & Emler, N. (June, 2007). Attitudes, values and moral reasoning as predictors of delinquency. *British Journal of Developmental Psychology, 25*(2), 169-183.

Tertilt, H. (1996). *Turkish power boys.* Frankfurt/Main: Suhrkamp.

Thompson, K. (June, 2008). Keeping it real: Reality and representation in Maasai hip-hop. *Journal of African Cultural Studies, 20*(1), 33-44.

Took, K., & Weiss, D. (1994). The relationship between heavy metal and rap music on adolescent turmoil: Real or artifact? *Adolescence, 29*(115), 613–22.

Turner, V. (December, 1979). Frame, flow and reflection: Ritual and drama as public liminality. *Japanese Journal of Religious Studies, 6*(4), 465-499.

Turner, V. W. (1974). *Dramas, fields, and metaphors: Symbolic action in human society.* Ithaca, NY: Cornell University Press.

van Gennep, A. (1960). *The rites of passage.* Translated by Monika B. Vizedom and Gabrielle L. Caffee. Chicago: University of Chicago Press.

Winthrop, R. H. (1991). *Dictionary of concepts in cultural anthropology.* Westport, CT: Greenwood Press.

Chapter VII: Hip-Hop Pedagogy

I start to think and then I sink,
into the paper like I was ink. When I'm writing,
I'm trapped in between the lines,
I escape when I finish the rhyme.
Eric B & Rakim, "I Know You Got Soul,"
Paid in Full, 1987

Reach and preach, through music I'll teach.
Doug E. Fresh *All the Way to Heaven* 1986

Rap is rhythm and poetry.
Hip-hop is storytelling and poetry as well.
Ajay Naidu, interview, 2002

The Art of Being Cool

Introduction

While discussing possible proposal topics with a tenured professor for a presentation at the National Council on Educating Black Children's annual conference, it was suggested that we create a workshop using hip-hop as a means to help understand Black male students and improve student achievement. This idea was based on educational consultant Ron Kelly, who asserts that students are capable of memorizing every word of a rap song because of their extreme interest in rap music. Therefore, when academic concepts are placed in rap form, you get a higher level of student achievement because it appeals so much to their interests and is overall a "catchy" way of learning (Kelly, 2007).

Using hip-hop as a cool way to appeal to students intellectually seemed to be a logical discussion topic for educating Black children. Coincidentally, while reading "Historical and Sociocultural Influences on African American Education," chapter 23 of James and Cherry Banks's *Handbook of Research in Multicultural Education* (2004), culturally responsive systems for teaching early literacy skills to African American children seemed to be effective as well. Below is the result of that initial conversation and some research. This chapter will begin with a brief description of hip-hop, a short overview of misconceptions and negative effects of hip-hop as well as the reasons behind them, a definition of multiple learners, a theoretical framework, a literature review of hip-hop-inspired instructional strategies, a discussion of the findings with some conclusions, and a list of relevant websites.

Brief Description of Hip-Hop

Here in the United States, where hyphenated names are replete with cultural and ethnic identities, multiculturalism and the influence of multicultural education walks a similar path to hip-hop. *Hip* is a word traced from the West African Wolof word *hepi/hipi*, which means to see or to open one's eyes. The term came to the Americas when West Africans were captured and brought over on slave ships. "Hip is the dance between black and white—or insider-outsider that gives America its unique flavor and rhythm" (Leland, 2004, inside flap).

Hip-hop is a word coined in New York in one of the five boroughs called the Bronx in the 1970s by young African Americans, Latino Americans, Caribbean Americans, Irish Americans, Italian Americans and Jewish Americans. *Hop*, according to Alan Lomax, is a motion most commonly used by agricultural-based cultures in their ritualized dances (1976). Either by dragging their feet along the ground or by hopping—stomping—the foot into the ground portrays these movements in homage to

Chapter VII: Hip-Hop Pedagogy

African-descended people's digging and planting routines. In the inner city, hop can be viewed as individuals who "hop" off subway cars. During previous eras such as the Harlem Renaissance of the 1920s dances such as the Lindy Hop involved high-stepping stomp-like movements (Stearns, 1969); more recently, in the 1960s African American fraternities began to perform "steps," stomping routines as part of presentations for their peers at historically Black colleges and universities (HBCUs) such as Morehouse, Hampton, and Grambling State University (Bufanda, 2004).

Hip-hop started in the 1970s when a gang truce that included many of New York's adolescents was in place. A local D-jay, Afrika Bambaattaa came up with the idea of repositioning adolescents' anger away from gang disputes and into music, dance, and graffiti (Nelson, 2004, p. 45). The result was the emergence in neighborhoods of Harlem and the Bronx of groups such as the Rock Steady Crew, Bronx City Bombers, and Zulu Nation. Reinforcing youths' interest in Bambaataa's idea was inventiveness that included turntables becoming musical instruments and lyrics resembling the scat singing that had made jazz vocalists such as Louis Armstrong, Ella Fitzgerald, Cab Calloway, and Sarah Vaughan world-famous. For these adolescents of the 1970s, Reagan-era budget cuts in music education and after-school programs, along with society's lack of substantial replacements of programming, society itself influenced the emergence of hip-hop.

Negative Effects of Hip-Hop

From its inception to its very definition, hip-hop is not only multicultural it is also constructivist. However, because of roots in oppressive and hostile environments, hip-hop has been more commonly known for its negative associations with delinquency. Research on adolescence and music blames hip-hop for almost everything wrong with today's youth. For example, it has been suggested that adolescents who have school-related behavioral problems have a preference for rap [hip-hop] music as well as high incidences of sexual activity, drug and alcohol abuse, and arrests (Epstein, Pratto, & Skipper, 1990). However, researchers also note that adolescent delinquency problems may just be a result of behaviors associated with being an adolescent (Took & Weiss, 1994) and that music "is a reflection of the social environment . . . and simply reflects already existing adolescent sentiments back to the youth subculture" (Epstein, et al., 1990, p. 382). It may be that problem behaviors such as adolescent drug abuse and violence can be seen as risk-taking conduct to which adolescents sometimes turn to test their potential and prove their individuality, and not a result of the music. In fact, adolescent delinquency has been a longtime concern for social science scholars, before hip-hop began. It is important to remember that hip-hop is the result of delinquency based on disenfranchisement of adolescent youth, lack of opportunity, and participation in gang life, not the cause of it.

Definition of Multiple Learners

This chapter makes use of two types of multiple learners, students and teachers. The most common definition of multiple learners involves the use of auditory, visual, and kinesthetic styles of absorbing and understanding information. There are, according to Howard Gardner, seven types of multiple intelligences: linguistic, logical-mathematical, visual-spatial, body-kinesthetic, musical-rhythmic, interpersonal, and intrapersonal. However, according to NCATE, the National Council for Accreditation of Teacher Education (2001), which prepares standards for professional development schools (PDS) to use in partnership with professional education programs and school sites implementing the standards, the idea of multiple learners encompasses preschool-grade 12 students, parents, candidates, faculty, and other professionals that are involved in an integrated "whole-team" approach (NCATE, 2001). Multiple learners in this case also means educating the academy, the school, the parents, and the community in ways that empower them to be alert for culturally responsive ways that help students learn. This is strong evidence to support the concept that although hip-hop is most easily applied to the common understanding of multiple learners, auditory/rap, visual/graffiti, kinesthetic/B-boying and D-jaying, faculty, teachers, and parents can use hip-hop to stimulate students' interest in education—using terms and language that they are familiar with. In short, hip-hop can serve as a bridge between cultural praxis and educational theory.

Theoretical Framework

Based on its emphasis of using dialectics and interaction for cognitive development, no other theory is more similar to the essence of hip-hop than constructivism. With innovators such as Piaget (1950), Bruner (1961), and Vygotsky (1978), constructivist learners internalize and assimilate knowledge based on their experiences. This is also true for the nature and origin that created hip-hop. Research has shown that when educators use their students' background and cultural elements, students become self-involved, motivated, and responsible for their own learning (Lee, 2000a, 2002; Pinkard, 1999). Here the role of the teacher is to be a guide or facilitator of learners, not a banker who only deposits information. Dynamic and social, hip-hop by its very spirit and starting point inspires collective contribution. A constructivist approach to hip-hop pedagogy encourages students to examine who they are, what they know, how they came to know what they know, and what they can prove through the interplay of experience, reflection, and action—praxis (Clark, 2010). Because of both culturally and socially constructed misunderstanding of African American adolescent male behavior, such opportunities for positive interactions rarely present themselves.

Literature Review

Other groups, like American Indians and Mexican Americans, also perceive the assimilation of public schools to be detrimental to their culture, language, and identities (Ogbu & Matute-Bianchi, 1986). For example, from the first day of school Odawa Indians and Warm Spring Reservation Indians step into the classroom resisting cultural conventions of accepted behavior and practices that they feel identifies them as White (Erickson and Mohatt, 1982). Australian Aborigines (Bourke, 1993) and the Buraku outcasts in Japan (DeVos & Wagatsuma, 1967), view Westernized school curriculum as a subtractive process of cultural assimilation. This is strong evidence that cultures inside and outside of the U.S. struggle with the idea of losing their identities and cultural values in Western forms of education. Even Asian Americans, often mislabeled as the "perfect minority" tend to share a similar phenomenon as Black African immigrants; they have lower academic outcomes by the time they are third or higher generation immigrants who have become more Americanized (Kao & Tienda, 1995; Massey, Mooney, Torres, & Charles, 2007).

This research is reflected by another study that insists immigrant youths who identify with their ethnic group and are more traditional in beliefs and values have better grades and are more likely to go to college than their acculturated peers when they come to the U.S. (Padilla, 2004). Additionally, Southeast Asians' grade point average was positively related to high parental scores of preserving culture and identity in terms of living near people of their own ethnic group, and showing no interest in returning to their country of origin (Portes & Rumbaut, 2001). I take this to mean that ethnic identity that is inclusive of multiple realities and not just Black versus White dichotomies is the key to positive educational outcomes influenced by identity. White, privileged male norms cause overgeneralizations of the "norm," exaggerate the contrasts of between-group differences, and involve unrealistic evaluations of deficiency toward low status based on White as the control group (Padilla, 2004, p. 129). Based on the aforementioned dilemmas, culturally reflective approaches in the classroom are sorely needed.

Hip-Hop Constructivist Pedagogy

Research on using hip-hop and music in the classroom suggests that hip-hop constructivist pedagogy is culturally responsive and empowering for students. One reason for this is that hip-hop was created collectively by a group of culturally diverse adolescents.

The Art of Being Cool

The true essence of hip-hop is to enjoy it in groups. African American children in general prefer to work collectively and achieve well in groups (Boykin, 1983; Slavin, 1977; Slavin & Oickle, 1981). *Diglossia* or the appreciation of "high-and-low" languages (Saville-Troike, 1989) includes rather than restricts dialogue in a way that students from many cultural, ethnic, and social economic statuses (SES) can contribute. African American children tend to use nonlinear thinking in storytelling and interactions which derives power from Black English, language-expressive strategies. By working collectively in groups and facilitating structured conversations, this "cultural modeling" form of socially accepted learning styles among African Americans could eliminate the stigma of a student standing out for being smart (Lee, 2000b), or help African American boys balance their academic and social capital.

Hip-hop constructivist pedagogy is not restricted to language arts, but is useful with math as well. The Algebra Project, created by Moses and Cobb (2001), has had great success using culturally adaptive norms to improve young African Americans' advanced mathematics capabilities. This work is especially important since research suggests that taking Algebra I is an indicator for success in college for minorities (Oakes, Muir, & Joseph, 2004). By taking students on a subway train, often decorated with graffiti, Moses was able to engage in conversations with them using language they used in their own environment to make parallels in mathematics. A subway train route became a metaphor for a number line; stops along the way took the place of numbers on the number line (Moses & Cobb, 2001). If, for example, a subway train goes forward five stops (positive five) than goes back two stops (negative two) how many stops has it actually traveled? The answer is three (positive three). Hip-hop can also be used to explain fractions by explaining musical notations of whole-notes, half-notes, quarter-notes, eighth-notes and sixteenth-notes in musical notation (Moore, 2010). Music games involving students getting up and moving, stopping and counting on the beat, as well as having students tap rhythms on their bodies and hands are all examples of kinesthetic learning. Additionally, hip-hop constructivist pedagogy can be used to teach art appreciation. The shapes, colors, and symbolism in graffiti on subway cars and walls of buildings, for example, can be tied in with East African designs on homes, architecture of Dogon villages, statues from the Benin culture, etc., which can show students their dynamic/kinesthetic connections to African-influenced constructivisim.

Beginning with contemporary terms such as *throw-ups* (hip-hop graffiti in display on a surface) and *pieces* (hip-hop shorthand for masterpiece), educators can engage students with words and terms that lead to appreciation of other forms of visual art. Comparisons between classical art pieces and hip-hop graffiti

Chapter VII: Hip-Hop Pedagogy

can be made to illustrate how both culture and music combine to create art. Sometimes impressionistic, sometimes expressionistic, but always vivid, hip-hop graffiti can be used to describe, contrast and interpret many forms of art. This point of view empowers parents, the school, and the community with new methods of communicating with students in ways that can be culturally adapted.

Discussion and Conclusion

This brief chapter has argued that hip-hop is a cultural phenomenon that can be used positively and effectively to communicate educational instruction for multiple learners. Using constructivism as a frame of reference, the chapter featured a brief description of hip-hop, a short overview of the negative effects of hip-hop, a definition of multiple learners, the theoretical framework, a literature review of hip-hop inspired instructional strategies, and a discussion of the findings and conclusion. We mentioned that the four families of hip-hop, graffiti, B-boying, D-jaying, and rap are obviously related to auditory, visual, and kinesthetic learners. What is not so obvious is that hip-hop can be used as a tool for multiple learners at a PDS where faculty, teachers, and parents learn from and teach each other in cooperative groups. This allows both students in the classroom and the community and campus surrounding the classroom opportunities to engage in a culturally responsive dialectic. The evidence suggests that hip-hop constructivist pedagogy can be used to engage and involve diverse groups of learners in positive ways. This brief overview of lesson plans that use hip-hop as a form of constructivist pedagogy is by no means complete. It is suggested that other researchers continue and expand on the ideas presented above.

The Art of Being Cool

Helpful Websites

Educational Raps

http://www.educationalrap.com/

Rapping Math Teachers

http://www.edutopia.org/math-rap-hip-hop

Long Division Video & Songs for Grades K-8 by Mr. Duey

http://mrduey.com/

Teaching Character, Setting, and Plot with Raps

http://www.educationalrap.com/song/characters-setting-plot.html

Teaching about the Human Circulation System with Raps

http://www.educationalrap.com/song/circulatory-system.html

Flocabulary Beats, Rhymes & Science

http://www.flocabulary.com/science_listen.html

Using Hip-Hop to Learn U.S. History

http://www.flocabulary.com/historysample.html

Chapter VII: Hip-Hop Pedagogy

References

Banks, J., & Banks, C. (Eds.). (2004). *Handbook of research in multicultural education (2nd ed.).* San Francisco: Jossey-Bass.

Boykin, A. W. (1983). On academic task performance and Afro-American children. In J. T. Spence (Ed.), *Achievement and achievement motives* (pp. 324-371). Boston: W. H. Freeman.

Bourke, E. A. (1993). *Identity, Culture and Population* (unpublished paper).

Bruner, J. S. (1961). The act of discovery. *Harvard Educational Review, 31*(1), 21–32.

Bufanda, J. (2004). A brief history of step. Blackout. Medford, MA: Tufts University. Available at http://ase.tufts.edu/aso/blackout/history.html

Clark, C. (2010). *Theory and research in multicultural education.* CIG 662-001, Syllabus, University of Nevada, Las Vegas, 1-21.

DeVos, G., & Wagatsuma, H. (1966). *Japan's invisible race: Caste in culture and personality.* Berkeley: University of California Press.

dimmSummer. (January 23, 2002). Interview with Ajay Naidu. Ethnotechno. Available at http://ethnotechno.com/_content/ints/int_ajay_1.23.02.php

Edelman, M. W. (Spring, 1995). United we stand: A common vision. *Claiming Children, 1,* 6-12.

Epstein, J., Pratto, D., Skipper, J. (1990). Teenagers, behavioral problems, and preferences for heavy metal and rap music: A case study of a Southern middle school. *Deviant Behavior, 11,* 381-394.

Eric B., & Rakim. (1987). I know you got soul. Paid in full. New York: 4th & B'way, Island Records.

Erickson, F., & Mohatt, G. (1982). Cultural organization of participation structures in two classrooms of Indian students. In G. Spindler (Ed.), Doing the ethnography of schooling. New York: Holt, Rinehart, and Winston.

Gardner, H. (1993). Multiple intelligences: The theory in practice. New York: Basic Books.

Kao, G., & Tienda, M. (1995). Optimism and achievement: The educational performance of immigrant youth. *Social Science Quarterly, 76*(1), 1-19.

Kelly, R. (2007). *Edu-rap, volume 1* [workbook and CD]. San Antonio, TX: Konfident Enterprises.

Lee, C. D. (2002). Literacy, technology and culture. G. Hatano and X. Lin, Special Guest Editors). *Technology, Culture and Education* [Special issue of *Mind, Culture and Activity*].

Lee, C. D. (2000a). *The state of research on Black education.* (Invited paper.) Washington, DC: American Educational Research Association, Commission on Black Education.

Lee. C. D. (2000b). Signifying in the zone of proximal development. In C. D. Lee & P. Smagorinsky (Eds.), *Vygotskian perspectives on literacy research.* New York: Cambridge University Press.

Leland, J. (2004). *Hip: The history.* New York: Ecco.

Lomax, A. (1976). *Dance and human history: Step style, and palm play* **[videorecording]. Berkeley, CA: Choreometrics.**

Lusane, C. (2004). Rap, race and politics. In M. Forman & M. A. Neal (Eds.), *That's the joint! The hip-hop studies reader* (pp. 351-362). New York: Routledge.

Malone, B. (August, 2003). Chief rocka. *The Source Magazine: The Magazine of Hip-Hop Music, Culture & Politics* (15th anniversary jumpoff), *167,* 130-133.

Massey, D. S., Mooney, M., Torres, K., & Charles, C. (February, 2007). Black immigrants and Black natives attending selective colleges and universities in the United States. *American Journal of Education, 113,* 243-271. doi: 0195-67442007/11302-0004

Moore, D. (2010). Music math teaches order of operations using note values. Retrieved February 19, 2012 from http://www.lessonplanspage.com/MathMusicOrderOf Operations NoteValuesIdea46.htm

Moses, R. P., & Cobb, C. E. (2001). *Radical equations: Math literacy and civil rights.* New York: Beacon Press.

Chapter VII: Hip-Hop Pedagogy

National Council for Accreditation of Teacher Education (NCATE). (2001). Standards for professional development schools. Washington, DC: NCATE. Available at http://www.ncate .org LinkClick.aspx?fileticket=P2KEH2WR4 Xx%3d& tabid=107

Nelson G. (2004). Hip-hop's founding fathers speak the truth. In M. Forman & M. A. Neal (Eds.), *That's the joint! The hip-hop studies reader* (pp. 45-55). New York: Routledge.

Oakes, J., Muir, K., & Joseph, R. (2004). Access and achievement in mathematics and science: Inequalities that endure and change. In J. Banks & C. Banks (Eds.), *Handbook of research in multicultural education (2nd ed.)*. San Francisco: Jossey-Bass.

Ogbu, J. U., & Matute-Bianchi, M. B. (1986). Understanding sociocultural factors: Knowledge, identity and school adjustment. In California State Department of Education (Ed.), *Beyond language: Social and cultural factors in schooling language minority students* (pp. 73-142). Sacramento: Author/Editor.

Padilla, A. M. (2004). Quantitative methods in multicultural education research. In J. Banks & C. Banks (Eds.), *Handbook of research in multicultural education (2nd ed.)*. San Francisco: Jossey-Bass.

Piaget, J. (1950). *The psychology of intelligence*. New York: Routledge.

Pinkard, N. (April, 1999). Lyric reader: An architecture for creating intrinsically motivating and culturally responsive reading environments. *Interactive Learning Environments, 7*(1), 1-30.

Portes, A., & Rumbaut, R. (2001). *Legacies: The story of the immigrant second generation*. Berkeley: University of California Press.

Saville-Troike, M. (1989). *The ethnography of communication: An introduction*. New York: Basil Blackwell.

Slavin, R. (1977). *Student Team Learning Techniques: Narrowing the Achievement Gap* (Report no. 228). Baltimore, MD: Center for Social Organization of Schools, Johns Hopkins University.

Slavin, R., & Oickle, E. (July, 1981). Effects of cooperative learning teams on student achievement and race relations: Treatment by race interactions. *Sociology of Education, 54*(3), 174-180.

The Art of Being Cool

Stearns, M., & Stearns, J. (1968). *Jazz dance: the story of American vernacular dance.* New York: Macmillan.

Took, K., & Weiss, D. (Fall, 1994). The relationship between heavy metal and rap music on adolescent turmoil: Real or artifact? *Adolescence, 29*(115), 613–621.

Vygotsky, L. S., et al. (1978). *Mind in society: The development of higher mental processes.* Cambridge, MA: Harvard University Press.

Chapter VIII: Black Male Privilege

Wives, submit yourselves to your own husbands.

Ephesians 5:22, NIV

I got this African chick with Eddie Murphy on her skull
She like, "Jigga Man, why you treat me like animal?"
I'm like, "Excuse me Ms. Fufu, but when I met you're a$$
you was dead broke and naked, and now you want half."

Jay Z, "Girls, Girls, Girls,"

The Blueprint, 2001

Yo' momma so fat...

Pharcyde, "Ya Mama,"

Bizarre Ride II: The Pharcyde, 1992

The Art of Being Cool

Introduction

Being Black and male has a lot to do with appearances of being cool under adverse circumstances. In fact, ownership of being tough despite the odds is a part of being cool. Using cool to garner social and human capital is one of the few privileges of cool that Black men have. With her book *White Privilege and Male Privilege: A Personal Account of Coming to See Correspondences Through Work in Women's Studies,* Peggy McIntosh (1988) offered the world a new way of looking at privilege in a way that has inspired scholars to advance her ideas in distinct ways. Her second collection of essays *White Privilege, Unpacking the Invisible Knapsack* (1992), a working paper popularly known as Peggy's Knapsack, consisted largely of excerpts from the former book that focused mainly on White privilege. McIntosh's notoriety largely stems from explaining privilege in a way that makes the invisible and often easily deniable world of privilege obvious and communicable. McIntosh describes privilege as:

> ...an invisible package of unearned assets that I can count on cashing in each day, but about which I was "meant" to remain oblivious. White privilege is like an invisible weightless knapsack of special provisions, maps, passports, codebooks, visas, clothes, tools, and blank checks. (McIntosh, 1988, p. 1)

From this definition of "White privilege," discussion about other types of privilege and privilege in general becomes possible, because they can be described in ways that are easily understood.

Fairchild (2009) built on McIntosh's notions of White privilege and asserts that privilege pertains not only to race and gender, but also *religion.* Passed on to her as a Christian person, Christian privilege "is not necessarily earned but conferred" (Fairchild, 2009, p. 5). Lewis (2010) and Woods (2008) also expanded on McIntosh in yet another way with Black male privilege or BMP. Lewis, as quoted by Armah, said, "A working definition of Black male privilege is a system of built-in and often overlooked systematic advantages that center the experiences and concerns of Black men while minimizing the power that Black males hold" (Armah, 2010, p. 12).

Definition of BMP

Black Male Privilege, or BMP, at first glance appears to be insubstantial, intangible, and therefore inconsequential, because

Chapter VIII: Black Male Privilege

it does not seem to be based in reality. When Black men first hear the phrase, many of them ask, "How in the world can we as Black men be privileged in the United States?" What usually follows is a conversation on the statistically high numbers of unemployed Black men in the United States, the high accusation rate and conviction rate of Black men, a Black male imprisonment rate that is seven times higher than White males between the ages of 20 and 39 (Dyson, 2007), and the fact that more than 70% of African American households are run by single Black women (Hymowitz, 2005; Morgan, 1999). If there is Black male privilege, what then would African American males have to feel resentful toward? Wouldn't the existence of privilege negate the need to express a lack of control over one's destiny and well-being? Rap music especially reflects a rebellion against society's attempts to control Black masculinity in the home and on the street (Blair, 2004). One Black male in the award-winning documentary of gang members in South Los Angeles, *Crips and Bloods: Made in America,* stated that the reason he acted out was that his mother was not around the house enough to give him the love he needed (Peralta, 2008). Because of economic conditions, the judicial system, and the absence of African American men living in their children's households, African American men have a particularly unique experience with male oppression in the U.S.

Looked at in this way, BMP may very well be a counter-narrative to hegemonic masculinity which offers a way for Black men to *be* in the world. BMP has been described as influencing Black male discourse, behavior, and action, including misogyny and mistreatment of gay males (Lewis, 2010; Woods, 2008). Unlike Fairchild, however, Lewis and Woods identify BMP but do not provide any philosophical foundation or historic understanding of how BMP is constructed. They offer only explanations of how it operates.

Purpose

The purpose of this chapter is to move beyond outcomes and to provide some understanding of the foundations of BMP and how BMP can be used to examine gendered and racialized perspectives. I assert that BMP is heavily influenced by religious patriarchy, especially of the type found in Abrahamic religions. Specifically, I contend that four religious narratives are the most dominant: 1) the creation of man first and then woman; 2) the expulsion from the paradisiacal Garden of Eden; 3) the curse of Ham; and 4) the command not to lie with a man as with a woman. Passages from sacred texts play a significant role in the lives of African Americans in a way that is separate and distinct from other ethnic groups. For example, African Americans in the U.S. are more likely to attend religious services during the week and pray more often than any other ethnic group (Pew Forum, 2009). Even African Americans unaffiliated with a church, synagogue, or mosque are three times more likely to say that religion plays a very important role in their lives (Pew Forum). Additionally, African Americans typically attend churches in which most members are Black (Wilcox & Gomez, 1990).

African American religious institutions are vehicles of empowerment and serve as counter-narratives to prejudicial social conditions and as a source of resistance to cultural assimilation (Ammerman, 2005). Therefore, it is valid to look at possible religious influences in both the creation of BMP and how it can be used as a tool for critical analysis. This chapter is important because it firmly anchors subjective intellectual conversations of BMP around the solid bedrock of the historically influential role religion plays in gendered identity through the frameworks of postcolonial theory and critical race theory (CRT).

Methodology

This chapter uses both postcolonialism and CRT to illustrate how BMP can be used contextually to examine race-gendered perspectives of the world. Postcolonial theory asserts, "[I]f the text is that which contributes to the perpetuation of an unjust system, it must be challenged" (Lee, 2002, p. 5). Abrahamic texts serve as the text for much of this chapter. CRT is especially adept at understanding how marginalized and gendered groups use culture as forms of resistance. CRT shifts away from perspectives that suggest communities of color as being culturally deficient (Yosso, 2005). Combining postcolonialism and CRT provides a suitable framework in which to examine Abrahamic religious texts to highlight how sacred texts are used to form conceptions, beliefs, and actions toward Black men and how Black men use religion to conceptualize, identify, and engage their own ideas of masculinity.

Terms

I use the term "African American" as anyone who is of African descent who also recognizes themselves as part African and American. "Black" is used to designate not only anyone who is a descendant of an African (including the West Indies, Puerto Rico, Cuba, etc.), but also individuals who were in America during physical enslavement and therefore were not allowed to be recognized as American.

Chapter VIII: Black Male Privilege

Religious Influences on Black Masculinity

In the following sections, I present a religious perspective that elucidates the relationship religion has with hegemonic masculinity, in this case Abrahamic religions. I then highlight how religion plays a role in the way Black males have been historically viewed and treated. I then follow with a brief overview on how Abrahamic religion is the foundation of current Black thought and behavior that defines BMP.

This chapter uses the Sapirstein edition of the Torah with commentary by Rabbi Shlomo Itzhaki (also known by the acronym Rashi). Rashi is largely published and accepted and is known for his inclusiveness toward different religious perspectives (Miller & Schneerson, 2002). For scriptural references this book uses the Bible's *New International Version* (NIV), which was translated from original Hebrew, Aramaic, and Greek texts by more than 100 scholars and was then tested by various religious groups (NIV, p. xi). The scholastic rigor as well as the practical testing among believers make this an appropriate translation to use, because the NIV rejects colonial discourse and advances the underlying theme and tone with cultural sensitivity. For references to the Qur'an, this chapter uses the Abdullah Yusuf Ali translation of the Qur'an. Ali was influential in opening the first mosque in North America and is therefore influential in the United States. In general, whenever there are specific differences relative to the Torah, the Bible, and the Qur'an, I will mention them. Where there is no indication, the narratives are relatively the same. This is especially true of the Torah and the Bible.

I would also like to add that I am a third generation member of the African Methodist Episcopal (AME) Church who attended Catholic school. I state these facts to allow the reader to recognize that I acknowledge my contextual privileges, and I am aware of the influences that Christian religion has had in my life.

Abraham, Father of Nations. One of the most prominent figures in the Torah, Bible, and Qur'an is Abraham, whose name means "father of nations." Since Abraham is one of the commonalities of Judaism, Christianity, and Islam, which use the texts of the Torah, the Bible, and the Qur'an respectively, these faiths are collectively considered Abrahamic religions. The creation of the Earth and Adam, the expulsion from the paradisiacal Garden of Eden, the Curse of Ham (which has been used to rationalize enslavement of people with dark skin and to lynch them), as well the commandment not to lie with a man are the four commonalities of the Abrahamic religions that are this chapter's focus.

The Art of Being Cool

While there are differences between Judaism, Christianity, and Islam, the sacred texts of each contain the five chapters of Genesis, Exodus, Leviticus, the Book of Numbers, and Deuteronomy. These five chapters are also commonly known as the Pentateuch. While there are other religions practiced by Blacks, Abrahamic religions constitute the majority of formal religious institutions for Blacks in the United States (Pew Forum, 2009) and around the world.

And God Created. Often beautiful in both its complexity and simplicity, some interpretations of Abrahamic religion have led to beliefs that "segregate the sphere of sacredness from the natural environment, thus assigning it to the level of a supportive structure" (Pattberg, 2007, p. 5). This ideology of man separate from nature stems from the first book of the Pentateuch, Genesis. In it, God created the first man in His own image from the dust of the earth, named him Adam, and placed him in a garden. "He [God] created him [Adam] from dust, then said to him: 'Be.' And he was'" **(Qur'an 3:59).** Adam was allowed to do anything in the garden except eat from the tree of knowledge of good and evil. In the narrative, Adam was given dominion over the earth, to rule over the fish of the sea and the birds of the air and over every living creature that moves on the ground (Genesis 1:28). "(Yea, the same that) has made the earth (like a carpet) spread out, and has made for you roads (and channels) therein, in order that ye may find guidance (on the way)" (Qur'an 43:10). Adam's first act was to name all the animals of the earth. Adam then named Eve "woman," whose name means *came from man*. Since Adam, the first man, was given authority to name all things, including woman, a common assumption of religious patriarchy and BMP is to believe that man has dominion over the earth and women.

As this interpretation of Genesis spread across the Western hemisphere, the perception spread that nature and other, uncivilized cultures are enemies that need to be conquered (Pattberg, 2007). In fact, it can be argued the impetus for colonialism was based on the idea that man has the authority to dominate the earth (Genesis 1:26). The question, "Am I my brother's keeper?" (Genesis 4:9) allows for the interpretation that man is not responsible or held accountable for the actions he commits against humankind. "I am not (here) to watch over your doings" (Qur'an **6:104). Both of these verses can be interpreted to mean that men do not have responsibility toward other men or their land.**

Understanding the European scramble for African colonies and the United States' subsequent concept of manifest destiny is key to discussing postcolonial theory. Postcolonial theory largely

Chapter VIII: Black Male Privilege

deals with the effects of European conquests of indigenous cultures (Ashcroft, Griffiths, & Tiffin, 1995; Said, 1979). In both instances, cultural assimilation of the European-built ideology of masculinity dominates the literature, language, and political influence of its colonized people. That includes those of African descent. In fact, it is this religious interpretation of the role of masculinity that, according to Lamm (2003) is embodied in the standard used to compare not only educational outcomes and measures of intelligence but behavior as well: the White middle-class male (Padilla 2004). As Paulo Freire (2000) has observed the oppressor supplies the oppressed with a model of manhood. This means that historically patriarchal, European models of the performance of masculinity have residual effects for African American males who exercise their BMP in the way they treat not only other groups, but African American women as well.

The link between religious patriarchy is most evident within an axis mundi. In Abrahamic religions, the father is known as the axis mundi, or sacred center that helps orient the world through structure and male presence in the home. Firmly rooted in the CRT perspective of culture, in this case religious culture, as a navigational capital orienting a way of being, the concept of God as Father is significantly important in a home that practices Abrahamic religion. In fact, commitment to family is considered a sacred responsibility (Dollahite, 2003). The Torah and Bible defer to the father as the ultimate authority (Deuteronomy 5:16) and Islam states, "The pleasure of God is contained in the pleasure of the father even as His displeasure is contained in the displeasure of the father" (Tirmidhi, Hibban, Hakim). Clearly the perspectives of postcolonialism highlight patriarchal perspective that the man in the home is to be considered the head of the household.

Expulsion from the Garden of Eden. The patriarchal treatment of women can be traced to the circumstances that led to Adam and Eve being cast out of the Garden of Eden. Adam was told not to eat from the tree of knowledge of good and evil. Later, Eve was tempted by Satan and ate from the fruit of the tree of knowledge, and she persuaded Adam to do the same. ". . . when they tasted of the tree, their shame became manifest to them, and they began to sew together the leaves of the garden [of Eden]" (Qur'an 7:22). God discovered their actions when He looked for Adam and Eve in the Garden of Eden and called, "Where are you?" Adam answered, "I heard you in the garden and I was afraid because I was naked, so I hid." And God said, "Who told you that you were naked? Have you eaten from the tree that I commanded you not to eat from?" (Genesis 3:8-11) "'Did I not forbid you from that tree, and tell you that Satan is an avowed enemy unto you?'" (Qur'an 7:22)

Adam said yes and subsequently blamed Eve; Eve blamed the tempter Satan, and Satan blamed God. Here we have the beginning of the parallel idea of responsibility and sin. Realizing that Adam and Eve must have eaten from the tree of knowledge in order to know that they were naked, God asked them who was responsible. Adam and Eve were then cast out the Garden of Eden, also referred to as Paradise. Adam was cursed to have to toil the earth with the sweat of his brow, and Eve was cursed with pain during childbirth. In the Torah, Eve was further cursed with "enmity" from Adam (Genesis 3:15), and a "desire [that] shall be to thy husband, and he shall rule over you" (Genesis 3:16). The Amplified Bible describes the "desire" as "craving" (Genesis 3:16). Before the expulsion, the garden was paradise; outside the garden was the symbolic, ungodly wildness of nature. This wilderness was to be trampled on with "one's heel" (Genesis 3:15), as it fought back against man. Adam and Eve's disobedience or rebellion from God's command led to their punishment of a life without closeness to Him, as they were now left to wander in the strange new world of the wild.

The questions surrounding whether nature—the *wilderness*—needs to be tamed and whether women need to be dominated are further amplified by the opinion that woman's lack of judgment caused the expulsion from the Garden of Eden. From a patriarchal perspective, the downfall of the human species is attributed to the sins of Eve. CRT scholar Tate (1997) suggests the concept of a woman empowered by God in a racist and sexist society is not only an unlikely idea but a radical idea as well. This introduces the questions: Should women be given a chance to redeem themselves through Mary—the second Eve? On the other hand, did Eve (as the archetypal woman) make such an irresponsible mistake that women should not be given a wide range of choices again? According to Abrahamic religion, God commanded man to rule over Eve.

Abrahamic religions also have a history of being oppressive toward women. For example, the Torah, Bible, and Qur'an firmly advise women what to wear (Deuteronomy 22:5; 1 Corinthians 11:3-10; Qur'an 24:31; 33:59) and describe women as being worth only half as much as a man (Leviticus 27:3-7; Qur'an 2:282; 4:11; 4:176). Additionally, women are instructed to submit to their husbands (Ephesians 5:22). Hebrew language requires not only a separate way to speak to women, but also instructs them to sit separately from men during prayer (Zechariah

Chapter VIII: Black Male Privilege

12:12-14). The texts suggest the father—who can only be male—should be the leader in the household. While the Qur'an differs in perspective from the Torah and Bible in its view of women as powerful in regards to her sexuality instead of being intellectually and morally helpless (Mernissi, 1975), the result of religious patriarchy is the same. In the Qur'an, "men have a degree (of advantage) over them [women]" (Qur'an 2:228).

The common root here is that the patriarchal treatment and perception of women found in BMP are based on the narrative of Eve taking the first bite from the forbidden fruit and then tempting man. The link between religious patriarchy and BMP specifically is enacted within the Black male community as resistance, struggling to find a voice and some semblance of control in the largely Black female-dominated households they occupy. Because boys must define themselves in opposition to their mothers in order to become men, mother-reared men will develop a disproportionately "oppositional orientation" toward women (Balbus, 1992, p. 211). Since mother-centered households are the norm for Black families, the rejection of the mother and all things feminine becomes an act of necessary resistance to become a recognized man. This in turn causes BMP when Black men turn to oppressing women to feel more powerful in both action and the discourse exemplified in venues such as rap music (Collins, 2004; Hanna, 1992). In fact, it could be argued that BMP is the entire purpose of modern rap music.

For Black men, many of whom are lacking male role models, they have constructed their own definition of Black masculinity based on what they expect from themselves to survive (hooks, 2004; Franklin, 1985). This definition of Black masculinity is often conceptualized as a *cool pose* (Majors & Billson, 1992). Cool pose, the appearance of being resilient, relaxed, confident, and emotionally detached (Hecht, Jackson, & Ribeau, 2003), or the cool factor (Bean & Ransaw, 2012) is the very nature of BMP: restricting displays of emotion that contribute to contemporary problems between Black men and Black women in relationships.

The Curse of Ham. Not only is *religious ideology largely responsible for the mistreatment of women, it is also the underlying root of mistreatment of Black men which persists today.* The European practice of slavery was largely based on the 16th century belief that Blacks were descendants of Ham, which according to select readings of the Bible *(Genesis 9:24-27),* allowed enslavement of those who had dark skin *(Goldenberg, 2003). Besides corporal punishment, lynching was also an accepted means of discipline and control.*

The Art of Being Cool

It should be kept in mind that lynching of Blacks was typically a Southern American Christian practice; however, in North America most of the early lynchings were of Whites (Feimester, 2000). In fact, in 1891, 11 Italians were lynched in New Orleans. At the time, some European Americans believed they were not only superior to Blacks, but also to most other Whites. Used as a form of terrorism toward African Americans, lynching was seen as intending to have a deterrent effect on ideas of miscegenation and was a systematic, violent process based on interpretations of Christian versions of the Old and New Testaments.

These interpretations centered on two streams of thought. One set of notions came from the Old Testament and focused on pre-Christian laws and customs that forbade intermarriage, especially among "idolaters" but also among nations with whom the Israelites were having disputes or were at war (Genesis 24:3-4; Exodus 34:15-16; Deuteronomy 7:1-4; Judges 14:3). The other set of notions came from the New Testament, where the rule of marriage within one's own culture held sway alongside the idea that a good and honorable marriage involved oneness with a spouse while looking toward closeness with Christ as the model to follow (1 Corinthians 5:12-13; 1 Corinthians 7:12-14; Ephesians 5:31-33; Hebrews 13:4). The connection to lynching is twofold. Lynching was a form of severe punishment for the "sin" of being one of Ham's dark-skinned descendants (and therefore inheriting his "curse"—see Genesis 9:25). Additionally, lynching was carried out in the open, among "good" Christian Southern Americans, often on trees found on church property (Douglas, 2005; Brundage, 1993). Those in the lynch crowd and those who chose not to condemn lynching were likely among the Americans believing they had a Christian obligation to forcibly reinforce the message that for African American males, emancipation had nullified their value and increased the threat of them as potential miscegenationists (Douglas, 2005, pp. 3-4).

The symbolism in lynching is worth pointing out here. In addition to the lynch mobs' open behavior—most of the time, those carrying out and witnessing a lynching did not disguise themselves—there was open desecration of African Americans' houses of worship. It was not uncommon to burn African American churches before and after lynching. This desecration extended to the trees from which those being lynched were hung. "Trees are powerful symbolic objects, [that are] universally associated with both sacred and profane myths and rituals" (Patterson, 1998, p. 36).

Chapter VIII: Black Male Privilege

Trees in Christianity are symbols of the cross on which Christ—the second Adam—sacrificed His body. As Douglas (2005) informed us in *What's Faith Got to Do with It?*, during the late 1800s to early 1900s (a primary period of lynchings in the U.S.), newspaper accounts included descriptions of preachers exhorting parishioners to assault and lynch "that wicked person" (Douglas, 2005, p. 3; 1 Corinthians 5:12). This is not to say that Paul, author of 1 Corinthians would have advocated lynching. However, it indicates the degree to which a number of people clung to biblical notions of punishment and sin, despite the contradictory results which included trees and Christ's crucifixion. There are additional reference points involving trees. According to legend, Adam's son placed a seed in his throat and when he died, the seed grew into a tree whose branches were used for everything from the staff of Moses to the wood used in one of King Solomon's temples. Also, the wood from the tree that was used to crucify Christ and placed on Mount Golgotha, came from the same spot where Adam was buried (Every, 1970).

Participants in lynching were sacrificing what had been before Emancipation their most prized property, a Black man, in a ritual to honor God's previous "gift" to them—slavery—and in turn, to gain His blessing. To them lynching was a gift exchange that brought magical transference of inalienability, common in cultures that value property and ownership of animals. The stock in this case was the Black man, whose value had petered out after Emancipation and, to their mind should be further sacrificed after death by burning his body. In many ways, lynching represents sacrificial purification by the lynchers who ideologically have no choice but to offer the victim's body as "payment" to preserve their way of life. Similar to the burned offering on altars, sacrifice and smell were seen as important to God, who seemed to be aware of scent. All offerings of sacrifice were to be placed on an altar and then burned with the blood sprinkled against the altar.

White Southerners' fear of losing jobs to Blacks and immigrants' labor brought the beginnings of affirmative action (Katznelson, 2005) which was originally created to protect Whites, not Blacks. Immediately after the Civil War, a free slave was feared and thought of as a domestic enemy, especially in the South. The common antebellum view of African Americans was as rescued and lifted from the wilderness and savagery through slavery, leading to the idea that Afro-Americans were unredeemable and unchangeable savages who were a threat to civilized Southern life, especially after they had been granted freedom. The surefire way to cleanse the Southerner and protect the Southern way of life was a sacrifice and offering to the Lord in the form of a lynching. These lynchings, and later the cross burnings after the end of slavery, were often presided over by clergymen. Fundamentalist preachers and Klokards (national lecturers hired by the Klan, most of them ministers) were involved in the conspiracy of lynching, invoking the Bible to justify Black subordination. These preachers not only tolerated the sacrifices of lynching but also actively incited many of them (Patterson, 1998). This gave legitimacy to the claim that the ritualistic sacrifice of lynching was done in the name of God.

Research suggests the ritualized cultural memory of slavery causes Black men to actualize their BMP of historical oppression as reason to be hyper-vigilant against appearing weak. Internalized residual memory of slavery is in turn expressed externally in actions of cultural resistance. The trauma of enslavement and lynching empowers BMP in at least two forms: hostility or indifference. Toughness, decisiveness, aggressiveness, violence, and powerful athletic prowess (White, 2008; Franklin, 1985) are all valued traits to Black men. These tough-guy characteristics are sources of cultural capital that maintain acceptable ways to deal with racism and economic oppression (White, 2008; Oliver, 1989). The rapper Tupac describes this perspective when he asks, "What can I offer her?" (Shakur, 1999, p. 87). He realizes that because Black women seem to have outpaced Black men in employability and economic earning potential, he has nothing else to give a Black woman except his cool resolve.

In just one example of the relationship between religion and BMP, the very nature of inhumane treatment of Blacks is largely responsible for African Americans being so religious. This idea is supported by the CRT perspective which asserts that there is a historical tradition of looking at religion as a means to interrogate racism and marginalization (Tate, 2005). The very subject that caused the oppression of Black men is what they have identified as their salvation: blackness. Thus, the skin color of a Black man becomes cultural capital and a form of resistance to all forms of oppression. This resistance is supported by the cultural affirmations of the Black church.

As I have discussed, African Americans have historically sought out religious services as a refuge against oppression (Ward, 2005), perhaps in response to the suppression of their indigenous religions. This provides evidence to suggest that BMP is a response to historic physical and physiological trauma of lynching. CRT scholars West and Glaude (2003) assert that Black spirituality has been central to resistance to oppression. The Black church, such as the AME Church, is one such example. In the Black church, Blacks have turned to what are sometimes spiritual and allegorical interpretations of the Bible, such as the Promised Land, as literal translations for physical freedom. Unfortunately, a literal translation of Abrahamic texts has caused the oppression of gays in a way that is both a form of religious patriarchy and a form of hegemonic masculinity.

Do Not Lie with a Man. The complete passage (Leviticus 18:22), "Do not lie with a man as one lies with a woman; that is detestable" ["detestable" is *tow`ebah* which means "abomination" in the Torah] is the verse used to rationalize homophobia. The Qur'an warns, "For ye practice your lusts on men in preference to women: ye are indeed a people transgressing beyond bounds" (Qur'an 7:81).

Seen in many interpretations of Abrahamic religion as a question of religious morality, gay and lesbian relationships are often subject to more resentment in the synagogue, church and mosque than in society. Postcolonial scholar Sugirtharajah (2001) supports this perspective, asserting that sacred texts are thought to be the inspired word of God Himself. Homophobia in Black churches in particular is related to the authority given to literal interpretations of Scripture that were historically made as a means of providing hope for physiological refuge (Ward, 2005; Douglas, 1999). In fact, research suggests that men who harbor negative attitudes toward gays often find encouragement and support.

Lemelle and Battle (2004), for example, found that among Black men, regular church attendance was significantly associated with more homophobic attitudes toward gay males. *The term homophobia, men's fear of other men, is generally defined as a defensive effort against being emasculated (Kimmel, 2010).* Consequently, homosexuality is hardly discussed within the Black community, resulting in the perception that men suddenly wake up and choose to be gay instead of acknowledging it is a process (Johnson, 2003). Additionally, African American men who are gay have faced not only negative racial conceptions of being Black, but have also been confronted with internal moral conflicts about being gay as well. This causes an even greater adherence to the performance of masculinity, in this case Black masculinity.

Physical prowess, more so than intellect, is the more traditionally regarded signifier of Black manhood. Any male who is not hewing to the masculine image of a fighter is thereby rejected as a man and shunned for being different or feminine. *Actions, attitudes, and behaviors are under constant scrutiny to be "masculine," but heterosexuals' choice of sex partner is the only accepted form of intimacy allowed within the Black community.*

The Art of Being Cool

As a result, Black men who are gay are forced to secretly deny their true feelings and carry out cultural "expectations *for* men while secretly submitting to their personal attractions *to* men" (Pitt, 2006, p. 257). Homophobia in the Black community and the reason that Black men—gay or straight—treat other gay Black men negatively is clear evidence of the negative influences of Abrahamic religion on the perceptions of masculinity.

Discussion

Based on the prevailing evidence of White mistreatment toward others, women and Black men, it may be natural to ask: How can Black men be privileged? The answer lies in the general tendency that privilege can exist without one's knowledge of it or by remaining silent when it happens. As Connell & Messerschmidt (2005) assert regarding hegemonic masculinity, masculinity is complicit when men receive benefits of patriarchy through means of culture, institution, and persuasion without enacting it. An example of this unrealized and unearned form of BMP is when Black men see other Black men commit verbal or physical abuse against Black women and remain silent.

This does not mean that BMP is passive or unintentional. Often BMP is durable and survivable when it resists hegemonic patterns of masculinity and presents itself as a well-crafted response to marginalization, class inequities, and media-enforced sexuality (Poynting, Noble, & Tabar, 2003). In fact, the BMP in Black masculinity can be understood as a form of protest when marginalized men attempt to claim power in Western countries where they lack economic resources and regional or institutional authority (Poynting, et al.). It should also be kept in mind that BMP is not just about lack of economic or opportunity privilege, but also about attitudes and behaviors toward others, especially Black women or gays. These findings are supported by Cline (2010), who suggests that most religions have, at some point in the past, validated and reinforced various forms of discrimination—racial, gender, sexual orientation, etc.—toward others. The overarching theme of religious patriarchy informs and helps create a separate but similar reaction to the oppression of Black men who in turn oppress other groups.

This suggests that patriarchal religious privilege, as well as BMP, is based on race, gender, and sexuality and how power is enacted between them. This idea is supported by Connell and Messerschmidt (2005), who attest that masculinity is practiced as a social action and can differ according to the gender relations of the social setting. This would mean the group influences thought and behavior more than the individual does. It could be seen as a form of collectivism (Wilder, 2001), in this case, a type of Black male collectivism. BMP in particular is a form of collectivism that is more than just being identified as Black. As Miller, Gurin, Gurin, & Malanchuk (1981) state regarding group identity among African Americans, group consciousness is just as much about dissatisfaction with the social and political position of Blacks. In fact, a term related to BMP, *bionationalism,* is used whenever Black masculinity emerges as an enactment against the struggle of White domination (Crichlow, 2004). Because Blacks are such avid practitioners of religion, it is reasonable to assume that BMP is an often unconscious, natural response to the physiological and emotional solidarity that religion can often provide. In this regard, religious privilege and BMP are very similar. But beyond the similarity, the evidence clearly suggests that Abrahamic religion is a strong influence on BMP.

Conclusion

Throughout this chapter, I have used postcolonialism to show how religious patriarchy serves as an impetus for hegemonic masculinity and influences the way the world understands and reacts toward Black men. The narrative about the creation of man influences the way men think of themselves in terms of their environment as well as how they treat others. Additionally, the question of whether to take responsibility to take care of the Earth or to subdue it reflects male behavior toward the world and others who are on it. The blame of Eve for the expulsion from paradise is at the center of the point of view of morality, intelligence, and the domination of woman as well as the need to control women or to recognize that women can learn from their mistakes. This also allows men who are aware of their misogynistic tendencies to realize that women can be autonomous and that since it was a woman who originally sinned, only through women can humankind find redemption. The Curse of Ham was a biblical passage used to justify slavery and as a framework on which to conceptualize and enforce lynching in the South. Finally, the Levitical tenet "do not sleep with a man" has proven to be influential in the way homosexuality is regarded and in hostility toward gays.

Postcolonial theory was crucial for this brief examination because it takes into consideration the colonizer as well as the colonized (Rukundwa, 2008). CRT's usefulness was its ability to highlight how culture can be used as a form of resistance against religious patriarchy and the dominant ideology of hegemonic masculinity (Yosso, 2005). Utilizing this combination of theoretical frameworks was specifically crucial to examining historical implications of BMP because it articulated BMP's construction based on a framework that moved beyond hegemonic masculinity and addressed cultural aspects of patriarchy based on religion. By stepping away from religious privilege in general and religious patriarchy specifically and embracing privilege in a way that addresses culture as well as resistance to power, BMP becomes a concept that is more easily conceptualized and articulated in a way that can help find solutions. At this point, I would like to suggest that any researcher who tries to combine the infinite myths, innumerable realities, and multitude of ideas of what it means to be a Black man is optimistic at best.

When we as African Americans look in the mirror through the veil of double consciousness or from behind a window with a religiously influenced frame, we see doppelgangers of ourselves based on our personal images of identity. These images are constantly shifting and changing and distort the true picture of the Diaspora according to our own experiences. This is similar to ripples in a pond when we move closer to a pool of water for a closer look and exhale. In other words, whether we are looking in a mirror, a pool of water, or another's eyes, we project and reflect not only our bicultural nature and religious tendencies, but also our gender, our culture, and our race.

This is a glimpse into the eyes that African American men use when they engage in looking at the world using Black male privilege (BMP). It is the hope of this chapter to give just one perspective of Black masculinity by using the sacred texts of the Torah, the Bible, and the Qur'an, of Abrahamic religions that can lay the foundation for interpretations of BMP using postcolonial theory and CRT as theoretical frameworks. Future conversations about Black masculinity would benefit from quantitative and qualitative studies of additional factors that may contribute to BMP, such as the influence of underserved Black males in the American education system on the school-to-prison pipeline or the use of the *N*-word.

Chapter VIII: Black Male Privilege

References

Ashcroft, B., Griffiths, G., & Tiffin, H. (1995). *The postcolonial studies reader.* London: Routledge.

Ammerman, N. T. (2005). *Pillars of faith: American congregations and their partners.* Berkeley, CA: University of California Press.

Armah, E. M. (May 13, 2010). Black male privilege? *New York Amsterdam News*, 12.

Balbus, I. D. (1992). De-Kleining feminist mothering theory? *Theory and Society, 21*(6), 817-835.

Bean, T., & Ransaw, T. (2013). The masculinity and portrayals of African-American boys in young adult literature: A critical deconstruction of this genre. (Re)constructing gender through global literacy practices and policies. In Barbara Guzzetti and Thomas Bean's (Eds). *Adolescent literacies and the gendered self: (Re)constructing identities through multimodal literacy practices.* New York: Routledge.

Blair, M., E. (2004). Commercialization of the rap music youth subculture. In M. Forman & M. A. Neal (Eds.), *That's the joint! The hip-hop studies reader.* New York: Routledge.

Brundage, W. (1993). *Lynching in the new South: Georgia and Virginia 1880-1930.* Urbana: University of Illinois Press.

Cline, A. (2010). Religious privilege: How religion, religious groups, and beliefs are privileged. *About.com: Agnosticism/Atheisim.* Retrieved July 26, 2012 from http://atheism.about.com/od/churchstate/p/ReligiousPriv.htm

Collins, P. H. (2004). *Black sexual politics: African Americans, gender, and the new racism.* New York: Routledge.

Connell, R. W., & Messerschmidt, J. W. (2005). Hegemonic masculinity: Rethinking the concept. *Gender & Society, 19*(6), 829-859.

Crichlow, W. (2004). *Buller men and batty bwoys: Hidden men in Toronto and Halifax Black communities.* Toronto: University of Toronto Press.

Dollahite, D. (March, 2003). Fathering for eternity: Generative spirituality in Latter-Day Saint fathers of children with special needs. *Review of Religious Research, 44*(3), 237-251.

Douglas, K. B. (1999). *Sexuality and the Black Church: A womanist perspective*. Maryknoll, NY: Orbis Books.

Douglas, K. B. (2005). A Platonized tradition. In *What's faith got to do with it? Black bodies/Christian souls*. Maryknoll, NY: Orbis Books.

Dyson, M. (2007). *Debating race with Michael Eric Dyson*. New York: Basic Civitas Books.

Ehrenhaus, P., & Owen, S. A. (July/October, 2004). Race lynching and Christian Evangelicalism: Performances of faith. *Text and Performance Quarterly, 24*(3-4), 276-301. doi: 10.1080/10462930042000312779

Every, G. (1970). *Christian mythology*. London: Hamlyn.

Fairchild, E. (2009). Christian privilege, history, and trends in U.S. religion. *New Directions for Student Services, 125*, 5-11.

Feimester, C. N. (2000). *Ladies and lynching: The gendered discourse of mob violence in the new South, 1880-1930* (Doctoral dissertation). Princeton, NJ: Princeton University.

Fernando, G. (1864). *Copperhead catechism: For the instruction of such politicians as are of tender years*. New York: Sinclair Tousey.

Franklin, C. W. (May, 1985). The Black male urban barbershop as a sex-role socialization setting. *Sex Roles, 12*(9-10), 965-979.

Freire, P. (2000). *Pedagogy of the oppressed*. New York: Continuum.

Goldenberg, D. (2003). *The curse of Ham: Race and slavery in early Judaism, Christianity, and Islam*. Princeton, NJ: Princeton University Press.

Hanna, J. L. (1992). Moving messages: Identity and desire in popular music and social dance. In J. Lull (Ed.), *Popular music and communication* (pp. 176-195). Newbury Park, CA: Sage.

Hecht, M. L., Jackson, R. L., & Ribeau, S. A. (2003). *African American communication: Exploring identity and culture* (2nd ed.). Mahwah, NJ: Lawrence Erlbaum Associates.

hooks, b. (2004). *We real cool: Black men and masculinity*. New York: Routledge.

Chapter VIII: Black Male Privilege

Hofferth, S. L., Pleck, J. H., Stueve, J. L., Bianchi, S., & Sayer, L. (2002). The demography of fathers: What fathers do. In C. Tamis-LeMonda & N. Cabrera (Eds.), *Handbook of father involvement: Multidisciplinary perspectives* (pp. 63–90). Mahwah, NJ: Erlbaum.

Hymowitz, K. S. (August 21, 2005). Black America's crisis. *Dallas Morning News*. Retrieved August 16, 2012 from http://www.manhattan-institute.org/html/ miarticle.htm?id=3339

Jay Z. (2001). Girls, girls, girls. *The blueprint.* New York: Roc-A-Fella, Def Jam.

Johnson, E. (2003). Strange fruit: A performance about identity politics. *TDR: The Drama Review, 47*(2), 88-116.

Katz, J., & Earp, J. (1999). Tough guise: Violence, media, and the crisis in masculinity [video recording]. Northampton, MA: Media Education Foundation.

Katznelson, I. (2005). *When affirmative action was white: An untold history of racial inequality in twentieth-century America.* New York: W. W. Norton.

Kimmel, M. S. (2010). Masculinity as homophibia: Fear, shame, and silence in the construction of gender identity. In Paula Rothenberg (Ed.), *Race, class and gender in the United States* (6ᵗʰ edition). New York: Worth Publishing.

Lamm, K. (2003). Visuality and Black masculinity in Ralph Ellison's *Invisible Man* and Romare Bearden's photomontages. *Callaloo, 26*(3), 813-835.

Lee, C. D. (2002). Literacy, technology and culture. (G. Hatano and X. Lin, Special Guest Editors). *Technology, Culture and Education* [Special issue of *Mind, Culture and Activity*].

Lemelle, A. J., & Battle, J. (2004). Black masculinity matters in attitudes toward gay males. *Journal of Homosexuality, 47*(1), 39–51.

Lewis-McCoy, R. L. (February 24, 2010). Yes Virginia, there is Black male privilege. *Uptown notes: The keyboard is mightier than the sword.* Retrieved March 18, 2010 from http://www.uptownnotes.com

Majors, R. & Billson, J. M. (1992). *Cool pose: The dilemmas of Black manhood in America*. New York: Lexington Books.

Mathews. D. G. (August 22, 2000). The Southern rite of human sacrifice. *The Journal of Southern Religion, 10*. Retrieved March 21, 2010, from http://jsr.fsu.edu/mathews.htm

McIntosh, P. (1988). *White Privilege and Male Privilege: A Personal Account of Coming to See Correspondences Through Work in Women's Studies*. Working Paper #189. Wellesley, MA: Wellesley College Center for Research on Women.

McIntosh, P. (1992). White privilege and male privilege: A personal account of coming to see correspondences through work in women's studies. In M. Andersen & P. H. Collins (Eds.), *Race, class, and gender: An anthology*. Belmont, CA: Wadsworth Publishing.

Mernissi, F. (1975). *Beyond the veil*. New York: John Wiley and Sons.

Miller, A., Gurin, P., Gurin, G., & Malanchuk, O. (August, 1981). Group consciousness and political participation. *American Journal of Political Science, 25*(3), 494-511.

Miller, C., & Schneerson, M. M. (2002). *The Gutnick edition Chumash*. Brooklyn, NY: Kol Menachem.

Morgan, J. (1999). *When chicken-heads come home to roost: A hip-hop feminist breaks it down*. New York: Harper Collins.

Oliver, W. (1989). Sexual conquest and patterns of Black-on-Black violence: A structural-cultural perspective. *Violence and Victims, 4*, 257-273.

Padilla, A. M. (2004). Quantitative methods in multicultural education research. In J. Banks & C. Banks (Eds.), *Handbook of research in multicultural education (2nd ed.)*. San Francisco: Jossey-Bass.

Pattberg, P. (2007). Conquest, domination and control: Europe's mastery of nature in historic perspective. *Journal of Political Ecology, 14*(4), 1-9.

Patterson, O. (1998). *Rituals of blood: Consequences of slavery in two American centuries*. New York: Basic Civitas Books.

Chapter VIII: Black Male Privilege

Peralta, S. (Director). (2008). *Crips and bloods: Made in America* [DVD]. Santa Monica, CA: Balance Vector Productions.

Pew Forum. (January, 2009). *A religious portrait of African-Americans.* Pew Forum on religion and public life. Retrieved August 16, 2012 from http://www.pewforum.org/A-Religious-Portrait-of-African-Americans.aspx

Pharcyde. (1992). Ya mama. *Bizarre ride II: The Pharcyde.* Los Angeles: Delicious Vinyl.

Pitt, R. (2006). Downlow mountain? De/stigmatizing bisexuality through pitying and pejorative discourses in media. *The Journal of Men's Studies, 14*(2), 254-258.

Poynting, S., Noble, G., & Tabar, P. (1999). "Intersections" of masculinity and ethnicity: A study of male Lebanese immigrant youth in Western Sydney. *Race Ethnicity and Education, 2*(1). doi: 10.4102/hts.v64i1.26

Rukundwa, L. S. (January 14, 2008). Postcolonial theory as a hermeneutical tool for Biblical reading. *Theological Studies, 64*(1), 339-351.

Said, E. (1979). *Orientalism.* New York: Vintage Books.

Shakur, T. (1999). *The rose that grew from concrete.* New York: Pocket Books.

Sugirtharajah, R. S. (2001). *The Bible and the Third World: Precolonial, colonial, and postcolonial encounters.* New York: Cambridge University Press.

Tate, W. (March, 2005). Ethics, engineering, and the challenge of racial reform in education. *Race, Ethnicity and Education, 8*(1), 121–7.

Ward, E. J. (2005). Homophobia, hypermasculinity and the U.S. Black church. *Culture, Health & Sexuality, 7*(5), 493–504.

West, C., & Glaude, E. (2003). *African American religious thought: An anthology.* Louisville, KY: Westminster/John Knox Press.

White, A. M. (2008). *Ain't I a feminist? African American men speak out on fatherhood, friendship, forgiveness, and freedom.* Albany, NY: State University of New York Press.

The Art of Being Cool

White, E. F. (1995). Africa on my mind: Gender, counter discourse and African American nationalism. In B. Guy-Sheftall (Ed.), *Words of fire: an anthology of African-American feminist thought*. New York: New Press.

Wilcox, C., & Gomez, L. (Autumn, 1990). Religion, group identification, and politics among American Blacks. *Sociological Analysis, 51*(3), 271-285.

Wilder, C. (2001). *In the company of Black men: The African influence on African American culture in New York City*. New York: New York University Press.

Wood, F. G. (1968). *Black scare; the racist response to emancipation and reconstruction*. Berkeley, CA: University of California Press.

Woods, J. (2008). The Black male privileges checklist. *Renaissance Male Project*. Retrieved March 18, 2010 from http://jewelwoods.com/node/9

Yosso, T. (2005). Whose culture has capital? A critical race theory discussion of community cultural wealth. *Race, Ethnicity and Education, 8*(1), 69-91.

Chapter IX: Black Grandfathers, Fathers, and Faith

He will turn the hearts of the fathers to their children,
and the hearts of the children to their fathers.
Malachi 4:6, NLT

Endure hardship as discipline; God is treating you as his sons.
For what son is not disciplined by his father?
Hebrews 12:7

I have always thanked God for making me a man,
but Martin Delany has always thanked God
for making him a Black man.
Frederick Douglass, ca. late 1850s

Men are not women and a man's balance
depends on the weight he carries between his legs.
James Baldwin, *No Name in the Street,* 1972

Do we have the willpower to believe that
We can develop Black boys into men?
Jawanza Kunjufu,
Countering the Conspiracy
to Destroy Black Boys, Vol. 1, 1985, p. 73

The Art of Being Cool

Introduction

When I was young I wanted to be like my mother's father. Grandpa Wilson was his name but everyone called him by his last name, Wilson. He was that cool—last name only. He wore the coolest suits and hats and he sat in a big green chair in the middle of the living room during family occasions, greeting everyone who came in. My grandfather had been a waiter back in the day when waiters had to wear tuxedos and knew how to cook right at your table. "How're you living?" was his catch phrase. My grandfather went to church every Sunday and "living" was a double entendre for both how life was going and whether we were living a spiritual life. My grandfather had a brother who had a shoe repair store. From them I learned about fashion, including shoes. I also learned about men's cologne, *Old Spice* and *Brut*, the only two colognes they used back in their day. My grandfather on my father's side used to take me on trips to museums. He worked in a post office, and from him I learned the importance of learning and a getting a good education. It wasn't until I was a little older that I wanted to be like my father. In other words, my grandfathers (and grand-uncle) were my first teachers. They taught me not only how to dress and cook, they also encouraged me to get a good education and go to church. They were just as involved in teaching me social and educational capital as my parents.

Cox (2006) reminds us that the Bible says parents play a strong role in raising children (Psalm 78; Hosea 4:6; Malachi 4:6; 1 Timothy 3:4-5). Grandfathers and fathers play important roles in teaching families about God. In particular, both the Old and New Testaments state the father is the ultimate educational authority (Deuteronomy 6:6-7; Ephesians 6:4). This is strong evidence that a father's religious attitude may affect the way he parents or the way he grandparents. In fact, some men become religious or even more religious when they become fathers (Nock, 1998). Often prayer, family dinners, and reading from religious texts serve as fathering tools to instill structure and establish a positive family life (Palkovitz & Palm, 1998). The problem with these research strains is that African American fathers are not typically viewed as positive fathers and role models, despite that fact that African American males attend church at least once a month (Patterson, 1998), and African American males tend to be more religious than any other ethnic group (Pew Forum, 2009).

There are gaps in research of African American fathers and their religious views of parenting. This chapter seeks to help close the research gap of African American fathers, religion, and parenting. This is particularly important because family relation-ships, pride, spirituality, and humanism are rated higher than traditional traits of power, sexuality, and ownership within the African American community (Hunter & Davis, 1992). Additionally,

Chapter IX: Black Grandfathers, Fathers, and Faith

Marsiglio, Amato, Day, and Lamb (2000) assert that parenting quality skills that are based on the cultural influences above, combined with a relationship with the mother and informal economic provisions, are the keys to positive outcomes for children of African American families.

In Abrahamic religions (Judaism, Christianity, and Islam), the father is known as the axis mundi, or sacred center that provides an orienting framework through structure and male presence in the home. Consequently, the concept of God as father—the ultimate axis mundi—is significantly important in Western culture. Individuals who are highly religious are known to value the importance of the father in family life (Palkovitz & Palm, 1998; Smith, et al., 2005). The divorce rate for highly religious couples is significantly lower than among the general population (Call & Heaton, 1997), therefore family stability increases with highly religious fathers. When fathers believe that family relationships and being a father are part of a divine plan, they are more likely to commit to marriage and fathering involvement (Doherty, et al., 1998). Groups such as the Protestant Promise Keepers, the Catholic St. Joseph's Covenant Keepers, and the Nation of Islam's sponsored Million Man March influence men to be responsible in matters of faith and family. For many men, the definition of fatherhood does not exist without a religious context.

Dollahite (2003) views fathering as a "spiritual process that each father works out in relation to his beliefs, his relationships, the moral call he feels from God, and the spiritual connection he feels with his child" (p. 3). The Church of Jesus Christ of Latter-day Saints (LDS or Mormon), one of the fastest growing and most family-oriented faith communities in the world has fathers believe in a divine plan that includes both the mortal and eternal life. Called generative spirituality, the men of the LDS are raised in a tradition that expects fathers to have an eternal relationship with their children (Dollahite). This gives them a tradition of caring for children. In fact, they consider commitment to children a sacred responsibility (Dollahite). This is a strong indication that religious belief influences the way fathers parent.

Theoretical Framework

Connell's (2005) writings of hegemonic masculinity argue that specific groups of men are privileged based on power structures such as race, gender, ethnicity and social classes more so than others. I take that to mean that masculinity of groups that are not privileged, such as fathers of African descent, require study within their own cultural constructions. A phenomenological qualitative study of fathers of African American descent will help recognize the cultural "power and privilege within masculinities, and recognize that masculinities are complicated and multifaceted and may even be contradictory" (Wedgwood, 2009, p. 336) to other forms of dominant masculinity. However, a cultural lens for understanding fathering is helpful only when the definition of culture moves beyond "ethnicity to include race, gender, sexual orientation, religion, and economic standing" (Miller & Maiter, 2008, p. 298).

Methodology

In an effort to understand the collective experience of African American fathers, this study used a hermeneutic phenomenological approach. The main research question was: "How important is religion to you as a fathering figure?"

Hermeneutics is a "research methodology aimed at producing rich textual descriptions of the experiencing of selected phenomena in the life world of individuals that are able to connect with the experience of all of us collectively" (Smith, 1997, p. 80). The word "hermeneutic" is a Greek term for a continuously reflective process with origins in religious interpretations. The hermeneutic process is interested in understanding an experience and involves fours steps: pre-understanding, understanding, sensitivity, and the fore-conception of completeness and language (Nåden, 2010).

Phenomenological research designs typically consist of interviews with up to 10 participants in an attempt to understand the essence of a phenomenon from the participants' perceptions (Hein & Austin, 2001). Van Manen describes phenomenological research as hermeneutic research to develop a rich or dense description of a phenomenon in a specific context (Van Manen, 1997). This approach typically involves an interview analysis or observation. Combined, the two interrelated terms of hermeneutics and phenomenology coalesce into a method that does more than just explain an event but understands its process.

Participant Selection

Semi-structured interviews were used to collect data on fathers' perceived views on changing roles of masculinity and their perceived influence on their children's educational outcomes. The data were based on biological African American grandfathers, fathers or African American stepfathers who were between the ages of 18 and 52. Eleven African American fathers were interviewed. The majority of the fathers earned between $25,000 and $50,000 a year. Most of the fathers self-rated themselves a 7 out of 10 as a father. Most of the fathers had at least two children living in the home.

Chapter IX: Black Grandfathers, Fathers, and Faith

Table 1

Participant demographic data

Name	Age	Children	Education	Income/Rating*
Howard	51	2	Master's	100+K / 7
Morehouse	42	2	Bachelor's	50-100K / 10
Fisk	40	3	No college	25-50K / 7
Clark	46	6	Bachelor's	50-100K / 5
Xavier	39	7	No college	25-50K
Hampton	47	1	No college	25-50K / 9
Grambling	42	3	Bachelor's	25-50K / 7
Wilberforce	47	2	Bachelor's	25-50K / 8
Jackson	37	4	Associate's	25-50K / 7
Morgan	74	10	No college	25-50K / 7
Bennett	72	1	Some college	50-100K / 9

At the start of each interview, the IRB procedures were clearly outlined, including the mention of a follow-up meeting where participants have the opportunity to look over the transcripts of our conversation to check for accuracy or to make corrections or to engage in a member's check at the end of the study (Merriam, 1998). Member checking is a "way of finding out whether the data analysis is congruent with the participants' experiences" (Curtin & Fossey, 2007, p. 92), and is best conducted when the interpreted pieces are presented as themes and patterns that emerge from the data and not just from transcripts alone (Creswell, 2009). Interviews did not begin until each of the participants signed the interview and audio interview forms. At the beginning of each interview session, participants were made aware of the purpose of the study and its goal: the researcher was looking for information on what African American fathers do to help their children get ahead in school.

The Art of Being Cool

The interview questions were based on Rubin and Rubin's *Qualitative Interviewing: The Art of Hearing Data* (2005, p. 143). While transcribing the interviews, vocalized pauses such as "uhh", "umm," and "ooh" were left out. After all of the interviews were conducted and transcribed, they were left for three days to clear my mind (Rubin & Rubin, 2005). This is directly in line with hermeneutic phenomenology analysis. A phenomenological qualitative study of fathers of African American descent will help recognize the cultural "power and privilege within masculinities, and recognize that masculinities are complicated and multifaceted and may even be contradictory" (Wedgwood, 2009, p. 336) to other forms of dominant masculinity.

Results

Participant Recruitment

Since African Americans typically attend Black churches (Wilcox & Gomez, 1990), it was logical to assume four separate religious and faith-based institutions would be the most likely place to find intersecting groups of African Americans with different incomes, ages, education, occupations, and family sizes. Baptist, Protestant, Walter Dean Mohammad, Nation of Islam, and one Catholic faith-based institution were the intended sites. These sites were selected from neighborhoods in Southern Nevada with a high concentration of African Americans (ERsys, 2011). According to the U.S. Census Bureau (2010), in 2000, African Americans were 9.7% of the total population in Nevada, and 7.5% of the total population in Las Vegas, mostly North Las Vegas. Many African Americans attend faith-based institutions, which includes religious community centers. The interest and response by officials at each institution were so enthusiastic that participants were recommended to me without having to post a single flier. The participants were selected from snowball recommendations.

At the beginning of each interview session, I clearly explained to each of the participants the purpose of the study and my goals. I told them I was simply looking for information on what can American fathers do to help their children get ahead in school. I clearly outlined the IRB procedures which included a follow-up meeting where they have the opportunity to look over the transcripts of our conversation to check for accuracy or to make corrections if necessary. I also asked them for permission to record the interview. Once the participants signed the interview and audio interview forms, I proceeded with the interview. Throughout the interview I allowed the informants enough time to answer the questions, however they felt fit. I interrupted or probed only when I needed clarification or more information. Although each interview was slightly different, I made a conscious effort to be hospitable, understanding, and empathetic whenever I could. At the conclusion of each interview, I did a short debriefing as much as time allowed. While transcribing the interviews I left out vocalized pauses such as *uhh's*, *umm's* and *ooh's*. In addition, I left out parts of the conversation that did not relate directly to the interview, such as instances where I attempted to build rapport and trust. I interviewed a total of 11 African American fathers living in North Las Vegas. Three were from a Methodist church, two were Sunni Muslims, two were NOI Muslims, one was Catholic and three were Baptist. Two fathers were single fathers, and three of the fathers were grandfathers. All of the interviews were conducted in the western part of the United States.

Site of research. The interviews and video clip reflections were conducted in the participant fathers' homes, coffee shops, library, and a community center office. Community centers are known to be socially influential in urban areas (Vidal, 2001). Just as importantly, research suggests that African Americans in the U.S. are more likely to attend religious services than any other ethnic group (Pew Forum, 2009). Additionally, African Americans typically attend churches in which most members are Black (Wilcox & Gomez, 1990). This meant that using local organizations and religious organizations both for participant recruitment facilitated the widest intercultural range of SES, class, and education levels of African American fathers.

Although a significant component, religion is not the focus of this chapter. African American religious institutions are vehicles of empowerment and serve as counter-narratives to prejudicial social conditions as well as a source of resistance to cultural assimilation (Ammerman, 2005). Therefore, it is likely that any sample of African Americans from most any local network location will likely include African American fathers who attend a religious institution.

Participants were informed that all interview materials will be kept in a locked drawer for no more than three years. Each participant was given a consent form to sign and told that participation was voluntary and could be terminated at any time without penalty. Each participant was also given a code number and later a pseudonym based on names of Historically Black Universities and Colleges (HBCUs). All data reported in aggregate form to avoid any possible identification in future publications. All data and recorded interviews will be stored in a locked drawer in an office in the Department of Teaching and Learning and destroyed three years after completion of the study.

The Art of Being Cool

Analysis

Ajjawi and Higgs (2007) describe hermeneutic phenomenology analysis as a process that requires at least six steps. Step 1 includes immersion; step 2, understanding; step 3, abstraction; step 4, synthesis and themes development; step 5, illumination and illustration of phenomena; and step 6, integration and critique of findings within the research and outside the research. I argue that fathering involvement by fathers of African descent has education outcomes that are unique from dominant forms of hegemonic framed masculinity.

Level 1. Open coded definitions: Prayer, family, blessing, religion, God, love, understanding.

Level 2. Data: Items, words, and phrases that seemed interesting and pertinent were highlighted. Interesting and pertinent terms included: grandfather, father, kin, structure, example, advice, religion, mom, gender, pray, affinity, mentor, teach, bonding, struggle, communication, model, media.

Level 3. Codes: The resulting interesting and pertinent terms were coded into nine categories: blessing, family, foundation, relationship, structure, strength, Bible, example, and plan.

Level 3. Themes: The nine codes of blueprint, structure, advice, affinity, bonding, emotion, struggle, communication, and media were analyzed to see if any patterns emerged. The remaining codes were placed into themes of fortitude, providence, and legacy.

Level 4. Testing the Themes: The themes of fortitude, providence, and legacy were tested to see if they reoccurred in a substantial manner during the interviews. Fortitude for the purpose of this chapter is defined as a sense of direction, a spiritual centering or moral compass. Providence is defined as the perspective that being a father is a blessing with responsibilities. Legacy is defined as something to pass on through example or as a standard or way to live.

What follows next are the interview profiles of each of the participants. I attempted to give a brief overview of each of the interviewees so that the reader would have some idea of the participants' background and to enhance the understanding of their personal narratives. Most of the fathers earned between 25,000 dollars and 50,000 dollars a year. Most of the fathers rated themselves a 7 out of 10 as a father. Most of the fathers had at least two children living in the home. All of the fathers were happy to talk about their fathering and shared with me their hopes, dreams, and fears in a most humbling, honest, and thoughtful manner.

Chapter IX: Black Grandfathers, Fathers, and Faith

Interview Profiles

Howard: Protestant

Howard is a manager of a telecommunications agency. He identifies as African American. He is 51 and earns between $50,000 and $100,000 a year. Howard has one daughter living in the home and one granddaughter living in the home as well. His daughter is 20 and his granddaughter is 4. Howard has an MBA, and was thoughtful, reflective, and talkative throughout the interview. Howard rates himself as a 7 out of 10 as a father, and identified with each of the three clips. His most memorable comment: "There's never enough time and there's never enough money!"

Morehouse: Protestant

Morehouse works with at-risk teens and coaches both football and basketball (but prefers coaching football). He identifies himself as African American. He is 42 and earns between $50,000 and $100,000 a year. Morehouse has two sons, one stepson and one biological son living in the home. His stepson is 19 and his biological son is 8. Morehouse has at least an undergraduate degree and was exuberant and excited to talk about his children and fathering. Morehouse rated himself a 10 out of 10 as a father and identified with the first clip focusing on the prayer. His most memorable comment: "They [kids] know who I am. I have their respect."

Fisk: Protestant

Fisk is a union representative and shop steward. He identifies as African American. He is both a stepfather and biological father, two of each respectively. Fisk is 40 and earns between $25,000 and $50,000 a year. He is a biological father of two, a 20-year-old daughter and a 14-year-old son, and is a stepfather to a 15-year-old daughter and a 7-year-old daughter. He has lived in the house with all of his children except his son who disappeared with him for four years of his life. Fisk did not self-identify as having graduated from college. Fisk was thoughtful, emotional, and pained throughout the interview, even crying at times. He rated himself a 7½ out of 10 as a father. Fisk identified with the fatherly conversations of each of the video clips. His most memorable comment: "I'm your parent, not your friend. But I can be friendly."

Clark: Baptist

Clark identifies as African American. Clark is 46 and earns between $50,000 and 4100,000 a year. He is both a stepfather and a biological father, with a 24-year-old biological daughter that is not in the home, a 23-year-old biological daughter, a 19-year-old

The Art of Being Cool

biological son, and two stepsons ages 19 and 16 respectively. Clark has an undergraduate degree. Clark rated himself as average as a father. He was patient and straightforward throughout the interview. He did not have time for the video clip reflections. His most memorable quote: "You can plant the seeds. Whether they take or not…?"

Xavier: Nation of Islam

Xavier is 39. He does not identify as African American because America does not offer African Americans the same opportunities as other Americans. He earns between $25,000 and $50,000 a year. He has four biological sons ages 14, 11, 5, and 2 and one stepson, age 11; he also has two daughters, a 22-year-old stepdaughter and a 2-year–old biological daughter. The 2-year-olds are twins. He is not sure if his oldest daughter is still attending college but he knows that she has enrolled. He has lived in the home with all of his children with the exception of his 11-year-old stepson whom the mother kept from him for four years. Xavier was very present and very pained throughout the interview. However, he was also thoughtful and reflective, even laughing occasionally. He does have some post-secondary education. He rates himself a 0 as a father because he states he has nothing to compare himself to. He says the standard of fathering is so high you can't even gauge it. He did not have a father in the home when he was young. Later in life he did have a stepfather who admitted that he did not know how to be a father to Xavier. He does not identify with any of the video clips saying this was because they were actors and they did not reflect reality. His most memorable quote: "The challenge to a man's masculinity is dealing with a woman while maintaining a position of dominance."

Hampton: Catholic

Hampton is the custodian and head of security at his church. He is 47 and makes between $25,000 and $50,000 a year. He is a stepfather and witnessed his stepson's birth. His stepson is 10. Hampton has graduated from high school and he rates himself as a 9 out of 10 as a father, saying there is always something you can know more about. Hampton was open and enthusiastic to talk about himself as a father. He modeled his fathering masculinity after his uncles, fathers, and men around him who took a special interest in him. His most memorable quote: "I can sense when something is wrong [with my son], I sense when he is feeling hurt, I can tell when he wants to talk. And that's a special father and son bond."

Chapter IX: Black Grandfathers, Fathers, and Faith

Grambling: Nation of Islam

Grambling is a direct Internet marketer who identifies as African American. He is 42 and makes between $25,000 and $50,000 a year. Grambling is a biological father of five, one of which is not by his current wife. He has a 16-year-old daughter, a home-schooled 5-year-old daughter, a 14-year-old daughter, a 12-year-old son and a 2-year-old son. He has an undergraduate degree and was poignant and humorous throughout the entire interview. He did not have a father in the home but modeled his masculinity from the male members of the mosque around him that took an interest in his mother. Hi most memorable quote: "I don't drink, don't smoke, don't chase women, don't chase men, so I aint't got no problems."

Wilberforce: Walter Dean Mohammad

Wilberforce is a 47-year-old business administrator, behavioral counselor, and business consultant and earns between $25,000 and $50,000 a year. He identifies as African American and is a biological father of two. His youngest son is 6 and his oldest son is 18. His youngest son is in first grade; his oldest son is a freshman in college. He has an undergraduate degree and was thoughtful with his answers as if he had spent a lot of time thinking about being a father. He modeled his masculinity after his father. He rates himself as an 8 as a father. His most memorable quote: "Education is an equalizer for African Americans."

Jackson: Walter Dean Mohammad

Jackson is in maintenance, is 37 years old and makes between $25,000 and $50,000 a year. He is a biological father of four, three girls and one boy. He has a 17-year-old daughter who is a senior in high school, an 11-year-old daughter who is in middle school, a 6-year-old daughter in first grade, and a 16-year-old son in high school. Jackson has secondary education from various technical schools. He did not see the video clips, and says he does not need a television to help him be a father or to learn how to be a man. He did not have a father in the home when he was younger and learned his masculinity from those around him which did not include his biological father who was not with him when he was young. However, he had a close relationship with his father which he still maintains today. He rates himself as a 7 out of 10 as a father. His happiest memories about being a father are birthdays. His most memorable quote: "I don't want pats on the back for what I'm supposed to be doing."

The Art of Being Cool

Morgan: Baptist

Morgan is a 74-year-old stepfather, father, grandfather and great-grandfather. He has 10 living children, including one stepson that he does not consider a stepchild, all over the age of 21. One son is deceased. He has 17 grandchildren. He states he has too many children to remember all of their ages. He has seven great-grandchildren, four boys and three girls, two of whom are twins. Morgan soberly and carefully detailed his experiences as if he had spent a lot of time in reflection about his journey form parent to great-grandfather. Morgan is retired, earning between $25,000 and $50,000 a year from pensions. He was awarded a sports scholarship to college, but was injured and unable to fulfill the academic requirements. He rates himself as too hard on his children, especially his sons. His most memorable quote: "A father should be a trailblazer."

Bennett: Baptist

Bennett is retired from the military and as a private contractor. He identifies as African American. He earns between $50,000 and $100,000 a year. He is 72 and a stepfather but does not consider the stepfathering as part of his personal definition. His 25-year-old daughter lives in the home, has just finished law school and is awaiting her bar results. Bennett has had some college but has not earned a degree. Of important note, Bennett has 11 siblings, six sisters and five brothers. All of the daughters have PhDs and all of the brothers have undergraduate degrees. He considers himself a 9 out of 10 as a father and states he gave too much. Bennett had very quick, short but thorough answers. He most identified with the Cosby clip because he and his wife sat down and discussed things with his daughter in the same manner. His most memorable quote: "My job as a father is to be stern, firm, and fair."

Theme I: Fortitude = Direction, a Centering or Moral Compass

"You might not have come into the world with the manual but we definitely got some compasses lying around" (Fisk). Here, Fisk sets the tone that became one of the overarching themes during the interview—fortitude or moral direction. Fisk recounted how he looked for direction on being a father and found it by examining his faith. Wilberforce would agree, stating he found his purpose through his spirituality. Bennett attested that he lines himself up with the word of God as much as he possible can, stating that as a father and as a grandfather, "I believe that I cannot preach one thing and then act another way." In regards to his fathering, Grambling tried to be an example to his children and his grandchildren. Clark emphasized that he could not have been able to do the things he had done as a father without God in his life, and Xavier tellingly lamented that religion was important to him as a father because "without [religious] order there's chaos." Morgan supports this viewpoint, stating that "without religion he would be lost." Hampton pushed the boundaries of providence to include religion and fathering as well as parenting, stating that religion is important to both he and his wife providing in spousal direction because the mother and father have to be on one accord.

Theme II: Providence = Grace—Being a Father is a Blessing with Responsibilities of Protection, Care, and Guardianship

Morehouse feels that religion helps a father protect himself when things come up, "and you need to arm yourself with the heavy armor [of God]." Xavier thinks that lack of faith as a father has been an overall detriment to society, stating, "If we look at the breakdown of family [and] the breakdown of our social structures we can look at it and see there is no religious order present in terms of a strict way of living that is designed to keep those things." Also, "There's a lot of Band-aids'® that I'd know Jesus did to help me and I'm hoping that I can make it" (Clark). Bennett seems to support this line of thinking: "No matter how hard you work or no matter what you do it's all part of [God's] plan."

Theme III: Legacy

Howard felt that a relationship with God was more important than just going to church. "It's not just about going to church on Sunday or participating in activities with church people, it's about what is your relationship with God (Howard). Both Grambling and Hampton feel that a strong relationship with God is something that is a necessary part of being a family. Grambling even went so far as to say that families that do not value religion have kids that are the first to fall off [the right path].

Discussion

Fortitude

True to the concept of axis mundi, or the viewpoint that a father is the center of family, the fathers I interviewed saw religion influencing fatherhood, the way a lighthouse beacon guides wayward travelers safely to shore. "Religion is what I need; it's the vessel to carry me with my family. Without it [religion] I'd be lost" (Morgan). Religion to the interviewed fathers' functions as a source of strength sent from God, and being a father serves as a spiritual bearing to his wife, children, and family.

Providence

Religion and fatherhood also functioned as a God-ordained ministry for the fathers of these interviews. "My study of how God wants the family to be and my obligation to family and being obedient to those guides is why I feel that I have the [positive] relationship with my family" (Morgan). Both as fathers and grandfathers the men I interviewed felt that it was a father's duty to be a religiously-centered father. This did not mean the interviewed fathers felt that instilling a sense of religion was the most important thing to being a father.

Legacy

The fathers I interviewed felt that religion is important but not as important to children as having a foundation or having a relationship with God. Often, "the first kids that are not highly religious are the first to fall off" (Grambling). The fathers felt that a relationship with the Creator was something important to pass on to their children. "Having God in your life is an important part of being a family" (Hampton).

Conclusion

This chapter asserts that African American fathers and grandfathers do feel that religion is important to their fatherhood. Specifically, in regard to the research question: "How important is religion to you as a fathering figure?" The answer is that they see themselves as men of fortitude, providence, and legacy. This is not surprising since the men in this study attend religious centers an average of once a month (Patterson, 1998). For many African Americans, religious institutions are vehicles of empowerment and serve as a counter-narrative to prejudicial social conditions and as a source of resistance to cultural assimilation (Ammerman, 2005). The church may be one of the few places that Black men and fathers can find encouragement and support. Given the fact that African American men are likely to attend church (Patterson, 1998), fathers often find support in the church (Ammerman, 2005), and fathers often become more religious after becoming a father (Nock, 1998), it is not unreasonable to assume that African American fathers interviewed in this chapter will be at least partly reflective of a larger sample.

Evidence of this is found in other research that supports the themes of fortitude, providence, and legacy. For example, Doherty, et al. (1998) not only asserts that fathers who are committed to being involved as fathers see it as part of a divine plan (providence), but Dollahite (2003) adds that religious fathers see fatherhood as a blessing from God and as a legacy to pass on to the next generation.

Take away

Throughout this book I have outlined how, at least initially, slavery was more about money than race. The financial reasons about slavery had a direct influence on African American males today. For instance, restricting African Americans from learning how to read as well as keeping them uninformed and unengaged had a direct correlation to Black males in American today. For example, many states create prison budgets based on how many Black boys cannot read in the fourth grade. I have also related how the link between the ability to have full access to society and education is so strong that many African American males have difficulty balancing the two. As a result, balancing ones' social capital with one's academic capital is the only source of empowerment that many Black males have. It is this safe place of emotional space the concept of cool becomes a sanctuary of self-reflection and empowerment.

I have also detailed how illiteracy and unemployment are two keys to American society that without either of them, Black males can find themselves locked in a pipeline from birth to prison laborer. It is the very disentrancement from society that made hip-hop. Part reaction against society part driving force of society, hip-hop gives a voice to silenced Black males who have few outlets of meaningful expression. hip-hop has become such a powerful icon of Black men that it simultaneously defines what a Black man is while simultaneously producing stereotypes about them. This artistic as well as discourseful, dichotomy spoken as both a victim of society and fully liberated creator of a new masculinity is part of the privilege of being a Black male. Empowering for both the listener and the creator, Hip-Hop that affirms Black masculinity can be a tool for educators to use for classroom engagement. Lastly, the final chapter encourages us to think of Black men as fathers, grandfathers and husbands. This is a direct challenge to the negative depictions of Black men and moves us toward a new direction of embracing them. What can be cooler than that?

References

Ajjawi, R., & Higgs, J. (December, 2007). Using hermeneutic phenomenology to investigate how experienced practitioners learn to communicate clinical. *The Qualitative Report, 12*(4), 612-638.

Ammerman, N. T. (2005). *Pillars of faith: American congregations and their partners.* Berkeley: University of California Press.

Baldwin, J. (1972). *No name in the street.* New York: Dial Press.

Bell, J. (1991). *Famous Black quotations.* Chicago: Sabayt Publications.

Call, V. R. A., & Heaton, T. B. (1997). Religious influence on marital stability. *Journal for the Scientific Study of Religion, 36*(3), 382-392.

Creswell, J. W. (2009). *Research design: Qualitative, quantitative, and mixed methods approaches.* Los Angeles: Sage.

Connell, R.W. (2005). *Masculinities* (2nd ed.). Berkeley: University of California Press.

Cox, W. F. (Fall, 2006). Parental educational responsibility: Is the medium necessarily the proper message in Christian schooling? *Journal of Research on Christian Education, 15*(2), 103-109.

Curtin, M., & Fossey, E. (2007). Research methods: Appraising the trustworthiness of qualitative studies: Guidelines for occupational therapists. *Australian Occupational Therapy Journal, 54*(2), 88-94.

Doherty, W. J., Erickson, M. F., & Kouneski, E. (1998). Responsible fatherhood: A review and conceptual framework. *Journal of Marriage and the Family*, 60, 277-292.

Dollahite, D. C. (March, 2003). Fathering for eternity: Generative spirituality in Latter-day Saint fathers of children with special needs. *Review of Religious Research, 44*(3), 237-251.

ERsys. (2011). Ethnicity makeup: Las Vegas, NV area as of 2000. Austin, TX: Synergos Technologies. Retrieved March 20, 2011 from http://www.ersys.com/usa/32/3240000/ethnic.htm

Chapter IX: Black Grandfathers, Fathers, and Faith

Hein, S. F., & Austin, W. J. (March, 2001). Empirical and hermeneutic approaches to phenomenological research in psychology: A comparison. *American Psychologist, 6*(1), 3-17.

Hunter, A. G., Davis, J. E. (1992). Constructing gender: An exploration of Afro-American men's conceptualization of manhood. *Gender and Society, 6(3),* 464-479.

Kunjufu, J. (1985). *Countering the conspiracy to destroy Black boys.* Chicago: African American Images.

Levine, R. S. (1997). *Martin Delany, Frederick Douglass, and the politics of representative identity.* Chapel Hill: University of North Carolina Press.

Marsiglio, W., Amato, P., Day, R. D, & Lamb, M. E. (November, 2000). Scholarship on fatherhood in the 1990s and beyond. *Journal of Marriage and the Family, 62*(4), 1173-1191.

Merriam, S. B. (1998). *Qualitative research and case study applications in education.* San Francisco, CA: Jossey-Bass.

Miller, W., & Maiter, S. (2008). Fatherhood and culture: Moving beyond stereotypical understandings. *Journal of Ethnic & Cultural Diversity in Social Work, 17*(3), 279-300.

Nock, S. L. (1998). *Marriage in men's lives.* New York: Oxford University Press.

Nåden, D. (March, 2010). Hermeneutics and observation—a discussion. *Nursing Inquiry, 17*(1), 75-81.

Palkovitz, R., & Palm (1997). Caring in contemporary families. In A. J. Hawkins & D. C. Dollahite (Eds.), *Generative fathering: Beyond deficit perspectives.* Thousand Oaks, CA: Sage.

Patterson, O. (1998). *Rituals of blood: Consequences of slavery in two American centuries.* New York: Basic Civitas Books.

Pew Forum. (January, 2009). *A religious portrait of African-Americans.* Pew Forum on religion and public life. Retrieved August 16, 2012 from http://www.pewforum.org/A-Religious-Portrait-of-African-Americans.aspx

Pleck, E. H., & Pleck, J. H. (1997). Fatherhood ideals in the United States: Historical dimensions. In M. E. Lamb (Ed.), *The role of the father in child development* (3rd ed.), (pp. 33-48). New York: Wiley.

Rollin, F. A. (1868). *Life and public services of Martin R. Delany.* Boston: Lee and Shepard.

Rubin, H. J., & Rubin, I. (2005). *Qualitative interviewing: The art of hearing data.* Thousand Oaks: Sage.

Smith, C. A., Krohn, M. D., Chu, R., & Best, O. (2005). African-American fathers: Myths and realities about their involvement with their firstborn children (electronic version). *Journal of Family Issues 26*(7), 975-1001.

Smith, D. (1997). Phenomenology: Methodology and method. In J. Higgs (Ed.), *Qualitative research: Discourse on methodologies* (pp. 75-80). Sydney, Australia: Hampden Press.

United States Census Bureau (2010). *Census 2010.* Retrieved from http://www.census.gov/

Van Manen, M. (1997). From meaning to method. *Qualitative Health Research, 7*(3), 345-369.

Van Manen, M. (1997). *Researching lived experience: Human science for an action sensitive pedagogy* (2nd ed.). London, Ontario: Althouse Press.

Vidal, A. C. (2001). Faith-based organizations in community development. Office of Policy Development and Research, U.S. Department of Housing and Community Development.

Wedgwood, N. (2009). Connell's theory of masculinity—its origins and influences on the study of gender. *Journal of Gender Studies 18*(4), 329-339.

Whitehead, S. M. (2002). *Men and masculinities: Key themes and new directions.* Cambridge: Polity Press.

Wilcox, C., & Gomez, L. (1990). Religion, group identification, and politics among American Blacks. *Sociological Analysis 51*(3), 271-285.

Chapter IX: Black Grandfathers, Fathers, and Faith

Appendix

Elements of Style

Ain't nobody dope as me

I'm just so fresh and so clean

Outcast

Ten Tips on How to Shop for, Wear, and Care for a Suit

1. Don't buy anything just because a female salesperson reco-mmended it.

2. Your suit tie and pocket square should never match exactly.

3. Your shoes should match the color of either your pants or your socks.

5. Your belt should match your shoes and the leather of your watch's wristband.

6. Your suit pants should always have a cuff, but tuxedo pants never have cuffs.

7. Wear pinstripes if you are short; don't wear double-breasted suits if you're portly.

8. Leave your suit out of the closet overnight to air out and to relax the wrinkles in the warm, but not hot sunlight of the morning.

9. Get a fitted suit (not bought off the rack) if you can.

10. Do not wear a belt and suspenders at the same time.

Ten Words to Know When Shopping for a Suit

1. Ablutions = a gentlemen's morning grooming ritual

2. Bespoke = tailor shop where suits are handmade from scratch

3. Pleat = a double or multiple fold in fabric that can be found on a pair of pants

4. Dart = a stitched or tapered fold that ends on a point sometimes found on shirt sleeves

5. Vent = a slit in a garment typically found on the back lower half of a suit

6. Coiffed = a well-done, stylish haircut

7. Haberdashery = shop that sells fine men's suits

8. Hang = whether you wear your inseam on the left or the right

9. Shod = appropriate and well made footwear

10. Aglets = metal tips at the end of shoelaces

Ten Tips on How to Get a Good Shave

1. Do not use the same razor blade twice.

2. Take your time!

3. Use sunscreen.

4. Use a post-shave lotion or oil.

5. In general, follow the grain of your beard.

6. Shave either in the shower or after so that your skin is moist.

7. Always use a fresh, clean razor.

8. Invest in a good razor.

9. Use a shaving brush to lather shaving cream or gel.

10. Use a moisturizer with a sunblock when you finish shaving.

Chapter IX: Black Grandfathers, Fathers, and Faith

Dateline of Ten Historical Influences on Men and Men's Fashion

B.C. - Ancient Egyptian pharaohs and high priests starch their formal wear, quickly starting an international trend.

1812 - Napoleon Bonaparte introduces buttons on coat jacket sleeves to stop his troops from wiping their runny noses when invading Russia during the winter.

1816 - Beau Brummell arrives in France wearing a simple but elegant black tailored coat and trousers, ending Victorian influence of men wearing heels and brightly colored scarves, ties, and suits.

1880 - The Oxford University rowing team takes off their hatbands and puts them around their neck, marking the birth of "preppy" style and the college tie.

1920s - The increase of women in the workplace coincides with the birth of the muscle man.

1926 - Hugh Hefner is born in Chicago.

1939 - Clark Gable says, "I don't give a damn" in *Gone with the Wind.*

1961 - A reporter asks for President John F. Kennedy's favorite books for casual reading. Kennedy includes Ian Fleming's *From Russia with Love* in his list. Ian's creation "Bond, James Bond" soon becomes legendary among readers in the U.S.

1972 - Francis Ford Coppola releases the first of his *Godfather* films; the gangster style becomes chic.

2009 - President Obama steps off Air Force One wearing a Hart Schaffner Marx suit.*

*President Obama also wears bullet-resistant suits by Miguel Caballero when the occasion presents itself.

Ten Fine Dining Tips

1. Slip the waiter a twenty when you first sit down and your level of service will improve.

2. Stay away from white zinfandels and white merlots; try a Riesling instead.

3. Germany's sparkling wines are almost as good as France's but for a quarter of the price.

4. Port wines come from Portugal; sherries, from Spain; cognacs/ Armagnacs, from France; whiskeys, from the States.

5. Pair wines with the preparation style; i.e., pair French wine with French food, Italian wine with Italian food, etc. Match the wine with the sauce, not the meat; e.g., a red wine can pair nicely with a seafood pasta dish if the sauce is tomato-based.

6. Sake no longer has to be served at room temperature; it can be chilled or even sparkling.

7. If you're ever in a restaurant and you don't find anything familiar on the wine list, it's perfectly fine to tell the waiter your top five favorites and ask for recommendations of similar wines.

8. Always be confident when ordering wine, but it's also okay to ask your date or dinner party guests what they like as well when ordering for the group.

9. At a dinner party, sometimes it might be a good idea to order two mid-priced bottles, one red and one white that everyone can enjoy instead of ordering just one expensive bottle.

10. If you get good service, tip accordingly. That means leaving more than 20% of the pre-tax total. They will remember you the next time you dine there or if you happen to arrive late or need a last-minute reservation. They will also be more likely to accommodate your needs for special occasions such as anniversaries or birthdays.

Other Tips on Fine Dining

Here are a few more basic guidelines. The laborious, ostentatious, and overly formal style of French dining service has long since faded away. However, there are still some basic rules to remember. In general, the silverware on the table coincides with the order of courses of a meal, from farthest away to nearest your plate or bowl. In other words, the fork on the far left and the knife on the far right will be your utensils for the first course (appetizer or salad). The same guidelines apply to wines; i.e., the first wine glass is on the far right. Usually, the waiter brings special utensils without being asked; e.g., a steak knife, crab cracker, demitasse spoon for espresso, etc.

Chapter IX: Black Grandfathers, Fathers, and Faith

Elements of Fatherhood

Toward the second half of the 19th century, fathers in the U.S. moved away from farms and small businesses to the emerging industrial economy, seeking work in big cities. This left the responsibility of raising children to the mothers and narrowed the perception of the father as one of breadwinner and provider. As long as the father was earning a paycheck, he was considered a good father and provider of a good home, making the single-parent earning income the accepted norm. Any man who did not provide financially for his family was considered a bad father.

This viewpoint of a good father based solely on providing financial support has negatively affected research and perceptions of African American males, who have unfairly become increasingly underemployed and unemployed. Consequently, African American fathers are historically and typically cast as poor husbands and bad fathers who do not do their part in rearing their children. How many of you knew the truth?

Ten Things About African American Fathers You Probably Didn't Know

1. African American fathers are more likely to help with domestic chores such as cooking and changing diapers than any other ethnic group (J. S. Turner, ed., *Families in America: A Reference Handbook,* 2002, p. 22).

2. African American fathers choose not to let the media define them as men or as fathers.

3. African American fathers have their children take and send cell phone pictures of their homework so they can check on their children's progress even when the fathers have to work late.

4. African American fathers often learn to parent based on what *not* to do when raised by absentee or uninvolved fathers.

5. African American fathers in the home are less likely to have sons who repeat a grade and less likely to have daughters who suffer from depression (National Fatherhood Initiative, The Father Factor, 2010).

6. Twenty-one percent of African American fathers marry and live with their child's mother within a decade of a premarital birth (R. B. Coles & C. Green, Eds., *Myth of the Missing Black Father,* 2009).

173

7. African American fathers pass on social capital in their parenting strategies.

8. African American fathers often treat their stepchildren as their own natural-born children.

9. African American fathers understand that a relationship with their children's mother is important to their success as a father.

10. African American fathers become more religious after the birth of their first child (Pew Forum, *A Religious Portrait of African-Americans,* 2009).

Elemental Education

Ten Things Minoritized Students Can Do to Be Successful in College

1. Meet your professors.

2. Remember you are not invisible.

3. Hand in assignments early or if you are unsure.

4. Read the syllabus.

5. Look at your professor's feedback, rewrite your paper, and resubmit it.

6. Read the book *BEFORE* you come to class.

7. Spend at least two hours per week on homework for every hour in class.

8. Remember that what you did in high school may not be enough for success in college.

9. Join an organization.

10. Read *The New York Times* or *Wall Street Journal* at least once a week.

Chapter IX: Black Grandfathers, Fathers, and Faith

In addition...

Meet your professors before or after the first class. Professors like to get to know their students. Meeting a professor and establishing an academic relationship early can benefit you in the long run when you need advice on courses you should take or when you need a letter of recommendation.

Remember that you are not invisible. Minoritized students often feel transparent attending a primarily White institution. When you feel unnoticed, you are more likely to come to class late, unable to relax your posture when you get to class, and you are less likely to speak up during discussions. Professors remember students who frequently come to class late, slouch, fall asleep and act uninterested in class. Those unconscious behaviors, coupled with a lack of class participation make it look as if you don't care and that you are taking your education and your professors for granted. Instead, come to class early, and have your books and notes open and ready to go when class starts, especially when you are a minoritized student. Colleges and universities are always asking professors for student recognition awards, and grant and scholarship recommendations. Looking like you are a well prepared and serious student can go a long way in your college career.

Hand in assignments early or if you are unsure. The first paper you hand in to a professor needs to be the best it can be. Establish an "A" student reputation at the beginning. Asking a professor to look over your paper before it's due or to ask for feedback on your outline before you write the paper just makes good sense. It establishes you as a student concerned about your grade and cuts down lots of work later on.

Read the syllabus. A syllabus is tedious and sometimes boring; many students just take a cursory glance at it. But reading a syllabus carefully will help you know and understand what the professor expects from students. Many times when students say something is unclear, that they didn't understand or miss an assignment, a good look at the syllabus would have solved the problem.

Every student becomes challenged at least once in college. Think about it; that's what college is for. In college, you're supposed to work on and learn new things. Minoritized students often take professors' comments personally. It is not uncommon for a minority student to feel "Is it because he doesn't understand me or my culture?" or "Did I get a bad grade because he doesn't like what I look like?" I know many White professors who go to lectures by minoritized authors, writers, and poets regularly and have professional relationships with them. "I went to school with so-and-so," some White professors will remark, or "Yeah, so-and-so was my first grad student." And it's almost impossible to tell a *hip*

White instructor just based on appearance. So, sometimes a professor is a professor because they are experts in their field and may have read more about the topic than what you might think. Look at your professors' feedback, rewrite your paper, and resubmit it. Even if the professor won't accept a rewritten paper, (most professors do) rewriting the paper based on their comments can become a guideline for a paper you have to submit to that professor in the future.

Read the book *BEFORE* you come to class. College is too complicated to come to class and then read the book. College professors already expect you to be able to read and understand a textbook, and don't want to spend as much time going over material that you should have read earlier. A good college will take the textbook and help you apply it in ways that you hadn't thought about. If you don't read the book before you come to class, the connections that your professor makes won't make sense.

Spend at least two hours per week on homework for every hour in class. When I was in school, I used to think the "smart" kids were the ones that didn't have to study. I thought that good grades just came easily to many White students. One day I realized the so-called "smart" students weren't smarter than me, they were out-studying me. Reading the book, going to class, and spending two hours a week on homework for every hour in class consistently is what gets you good grades in college. This study ratio, done consistently prevents trying to write entire term papers the night before they are due, helps prevent all-night study sessions, and allows you to schedule time for fun. In short, good college students find success through hard work.

Remember that what you did in high school may not be enough for success in college. College professors expect a lot from their students, and many minoritized students are not used to that level of expectation. High school mainly focuses on providing you with basic skills and helping you understand general concepts. Think high school = lesson, read, and repeat. College is all about putting things together, making connections, and providing clear explanations of your views and knowledge. Think college = read, lecture, support your thoughts convincingly. College professors rarely grade you on how they feel about your opinion. They grade you on how well supported your ideas are.

Join an organization. College challenges you to explore new experiences! The ability to adapt to change makes you a well-rounded individual. Being well-rounded will help you to connect to people easier and become a better candidate for internships and jobs. It doesn't have to be a sorority or a fraternity; joining any college organization can help you make crucial job-related contacts in the future.

Chapter IX: Black Grandfathers, Fathers, and Faith

Read *The New York Times* or *Wall Street Journal* at least once a week. Reading a good-quality paper not only helps you to be well-rounded and aware, it helps you be a better student. The more information you have, the better. Using a recent, relevant quote from credible news sources makes for stronger arguments in your papers. It also just plain makes you look smart.

Top Five Things to Do for Graduate School

1. Present at and attend conferences. I used to think that presenting at conferences was about highlighting research. Now I know that presenting at conferences is all about getting feedback that will help get you published. In addition, conferences are good places to find academic journal editors who might be interested in your work. Conferences are also places where you can find out the latest trends in research and expose yourself to new ideas. I've also seen prospective candidates or students who are about to graduate use opportunities to introduce themselves to potential job seekers. Conferences are also great places to network among your peers.

2. Choose your thesis or dissertation committee by being open-minded. Having a general idea about your final project is a great start. However, informal conversations with a professor in an elevator can spark ideas that may lead you to a more rewarding path. It pays to talk to as many professionals as you can about your interests. The feedback you get may be something you may not have thought of sparked by someone you never knew shared your interests.

3. If you're working on your dissertation, file for IRB (Institutional Review Board). This governing body allows you to conduct research as soon as you have defended your proposal and gotten approval to proceed from your dissertation committee. Starting the process as soon as possible cuts down on processing time, and if you need to make changes it's easier to update than to start over.

4. Start looking for a job as soon as your thesis prospectus is approved or your IRB is submitted. Seeing what types of jobs are currently available may make you refine your thesis or dissertation. Make sure that you have classes on your transcript that reflect the type of job you want to land when you graduate as well as add clout to your thesis or dissertation. Save cool ideas, research that is not specifically related to your impending job and your personal research interests until after you get hired. Your cover letter, vita, statement of teaching philosophy, research agenda, references, and transcripts must all align with the job. State in your cover letter how you fulfill the requirements in the job announcement in a way that your vita supports (with the items you mention at the beginning of the vita) and all of your other submission materials are in the same order as mentioned in the cover letter.

5. When listing references for jobs, don't just pick members of your thesis or dissertation committee. Some prospective employers want to know about your experience in the classroom, some may want to know your experience with supervising other graduate students, and some may want to know your experience with fellowships, internships, or summer jobs—these are items that not everyone on your dissertation committee would necessarily know about you. It may be a good idea to include one reference that is familiar with your research or you as a researcher, one who has witnessed you teach a class or be a teaching mentor, and one reference from a supervisor at a fellowship, internship, or other such program or summer job.

A Final Word

America started with settlers who had grown up on the ideas of manifest destiny and men who tamed the wild. Robin Hood and King Arthur's Crusades were stories that early male immigrants spoke out loud and sung in their hearts. In the 1800s, the prototypical masculine was Jesse James and Wyatt Earp. In the early 1900s, Irish immigrants re-interpreted the tough, self-reliant male as a slightly better dressed but not much more refined gansta': think Al Capone. (Yes, Capone is an Irish name.) In the 1930s, Italian immigrants re-interpreted masculinity as a more glamorized, visible type of well-dressed hooligan à la Bugsy Siegel, the celebrity gansta'. In the 1980s, popular culture's version of this gangster style emerged, following the box office success in 1977 of the film *Saturday Night Fever*. This was followed by the gangsta' image of a rapper, widely accepted as an African American male. Now both Black guys and White guys wear do-rags and saggy pants.

What does all this say about the changes in American masculinity? It's not an ethnicity that men are trying to copy. Masculinity is about what is and isn't a socially accepted performance of masculinity. So don't get hung up on race; men of every culture want to be tough and in control.